LET'S LEARN PRAYER

by SOL SCHARFSTEIN

KTAV PUBLISHING HOUSE, INC.

COPYRIGHT © 1985

KTAV PUBLISHING HOUSE INC.
ISBN 0-88125-189-5
MV86

הַתֹּכֶן

8 הַמּוֹצִיא
15 בִּרְכַּת הַמָּזוֹן
22 בִּרְכַּת הַנֵּרוֹת לְשַׁבָּת
30 קִדּוּשׁ
36 לְכָה דוֹדִי
41 שְׁמַע
48 וְאָהַבְתָּ אֵת־יְיָ אֱלֹהֶךָ
55 מִי־כָמוֹכָה
64 וְשָׁמְרוּ בְנֵי יִשְׂרָאֵל אֶת הַשַּׁבָּת
70 עָלֵינוּ
78 אֵין כֵּאלֹהֵינוּ
87 יְבָרֶכְךָ יְיָ
93 מַה־טֹּבוּ אֹהָלֶיךָ
102 יוֹצֵר הַמְּאוֹרוֹת
109 קְדוּשָּׁה
114 הוֹצָאַת הַתּוֹרָה
120 בָּרְכוּ אֶת־יְיָ
125 נוֹתֵן הַתּוֹרָה
131 תּוֹרַת אֱמֶת
139 עֵץ חַיִּים הִיא
145 הַבְדָּלָה
153 Siddur Readings

INTRODUCTION

Let's Learn Prayer is a textbook-workbook designed to teach prayer not as an isolated skill but as a function of the total fiber of living Judaism: prayer, customs, Hebrew language, and grammar.

Let's Learn Prayer is divided into twenty-one prayer units. Each of these units is subdivided into four teaching sections, each of which review and build on the material already presented. These sections are structured to add to and enhance prayer reading, content comprehension, Hebrew language, and ethical and valuing skills. They contain:

   1. Vocabulary lists and "Knowing the Words" exercises to test word acquisition and comprehension.

   2. Prayer units phrased into Hebrew and English, preceded by a concise comment which provides background information on the significance, history, usage, and ethics of the prayer.

The translations are simple, comfortable, and convey the majesty of and reverence for the prayer.

I have endeavored to eliminate "sexism" from the translations to the extent possible. The necessities of teaching grammatical exercises and gender have precluded full success in this effort.

The "Phrase Prayer" unit is always followed by a comprehension exercise, "Knowing the Phrases."

   3. A repetition of the prayer which provides yet another opportunity to practice fluency and reading skills. Once again, the same prayer is preceded by a comment providing further background information.

The reading skills teaching section is followed by a variety of exercises in Hebrew and English.

"Knowing the Answers" focuses its attention on the prayer's moral/ethical content and the relevancy to everyday living.

"Knowing the Prefixes or Suffixes" teaches students to analyze prayer vocabulary for its grammatical components.

"Knowing the Prayer" tests Hebrew word comprehension and fluency of the students.

   4. The fourth section consists of Jewish value essays which highlight the historical, ethical, and religious significance of the prayer.

Each of these enrichment units is accompanied by a "value clarification" exercise designed to enable students to relate the contents of the prayer to their daily lives.

The skill exercises in *Let's Learn Prayer* can be performed without knowledge of Hebrew writing.

Let's Learn Prayer will be an enjoyable and uplifting learning experience for your students.

SOL SCHARFSTEIN

תְּפִלָּה Prayer

Prayer, תְּפִלָּה, is a way of talking to God. When you talk to God, it may be to say thank-you, or to offer praise, or to ask God for something for yourself or your community, but it must be done with *love*. When you pray to God purely and sincerely, it is called a service of the heart, עֲבוֹדָה שֶׁבַּלֵּב. When you serve God with all your heart, not only do you earn a מִצְוָה, but you feel good too.

It is certainly wonderful if you can talk to God whenever you feel like it, but many people have trouble putting their feelings and thoughts into words. That is why great Jewish rabbis, scholars, and poets wrote down their beautiful prayers (in Hebrew, of course!) so others would be able to say them to God. These prayers are arranged in a special order in the סִדּוּר, or prayer book.

The סִדּוּר contains prayers for the three daily services—שַׁחֲרִית, מִנְחָה, and מַעֲרִיב, morning, afternoon, and evening. There are extra prayers for the Sabbath and for holidays and special occasions. Our rabbis tried to write prayers to cover every possible event. There is even a prayer you can say when you see something especially beautiful in nature!

All of this was done just to help you speak to God. So the next time you have something to say, you needn't feel tongue-tied. Just open your סִדּוּר.

What Do You Think?

1. What are some good ways to say תּוֹדָה to God?
2. What do you consider the best way?
3. What can you say through prayer besides thank-you?
4. Have you ever talked to God?
5. What did you say?
6. When you pray from the סִדּוּר, do you feel like you're talking to God?
7. What are some things you could do to make praying from a סִדּוּר feel more like talking to God?

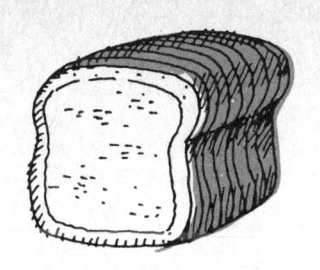

הַמּוֹצִיא
Blessing Over Bread

Knowing the Prayer Vocabulary

הָעוֹלָם	the world	בָּרוּךְ	blessed
עוֹלָם	world	בֵּרֵךְ	he blessed
הַמּוֹצִיא	who brings forth	אַתָּה	you
לֶחֶם	bread (food)	יְיָ	Eternal
הָאָרֶץ	the earth	אֱלֹהֵינוּ	our God
אֶרֶץ	earth	אֱלֹהִים	God
		מֶלֶךְ	ruler, King

Knowing the Words
Circle the correct Hebrew word.

1. earth	אֶרֶץ	אַתָּה	בָּרוּר
2. bread (food)	מֶלֶךְ	לֶחֶם	בָּרוּךְ
3. world	עוֹלָם	אַתָּה	מֶלֶךְ
4. our God	אֱלֹהִים	מֶלֶךְ	אֱלֹהֵינוּ
5. the world	הָעוֹלָם	הַמּוֹצִיא	לֶחֶם
6. Eternal	הָעוֹלָם	יְיָ	הָאָרֶץ
7. he blessed	אַתָּה	הַמּוֹצִיא	בֵּרַךְ
8. you	מִן	אַתָּה	לֶחֶם
9. who brings forth	הַמּוֹצִיא	בָּרוּךְ	אֱלֹהֵינוּ
10. ruler, King	הָעוֹלָם	הָעוֹלָם	מֶלֶךְ
11. God	בָּרוּךְ	אֱלֹהֵי	לֶחֶם
12. blessed	הָאָרֶץ	אַתָּה	בָּרוּךְ
13. the earth	מִן	הָאָרֶץ	הַמּוֹצִיא

We recite blessings to remind us to appreciate God's world. When we say a blessing we remind ourselves about beauty, wonders, and love and about God's place in our lives.

When we recite a blessing and thank God for one of the world's wonders, we feel good all over. We know that we have done the right thing and have added happiness to our lives.

Blessed are You, Eternal,	בָּרוּךְ אַתָּה יְיָ,
our God, ruler of the world,	אֱלֹהֵינוּ מֶלֶךְ הָעוֹלָם,
who brings forth bread (food)	הַמּוֹצִיא לֶחֶם
from the earth.	מִן הָאָרֶץ.

Knowing the Phrases
Drawing a line from the Hebrew phrase to its English meaning.

1. our God, ruler of the world,	הַמּוֹצִיא לֶחֶם
2. from the earth.	בָּרוּךְ אַתָּה יְיָ
3. who brings forth bread (food)	מִן הָאָרֶץ
4. Blessed are you, Eternal	אֱלֹהֵינוּ מֶלֶךְ הָעוֹלָם

There are group בְּרָכוֹת for all kinds of vegetables, fruits, milk products, meats, and fish. However, because לֶחֶם is the staff of life, it has a special individual בְּרָכָה.

All בְּרָכוֹת begin with the words בָּרוּךְ אַתָּה יְיָ, אֱלֹהֵינוּ מֶלֶךְ הָעוֹלָם.

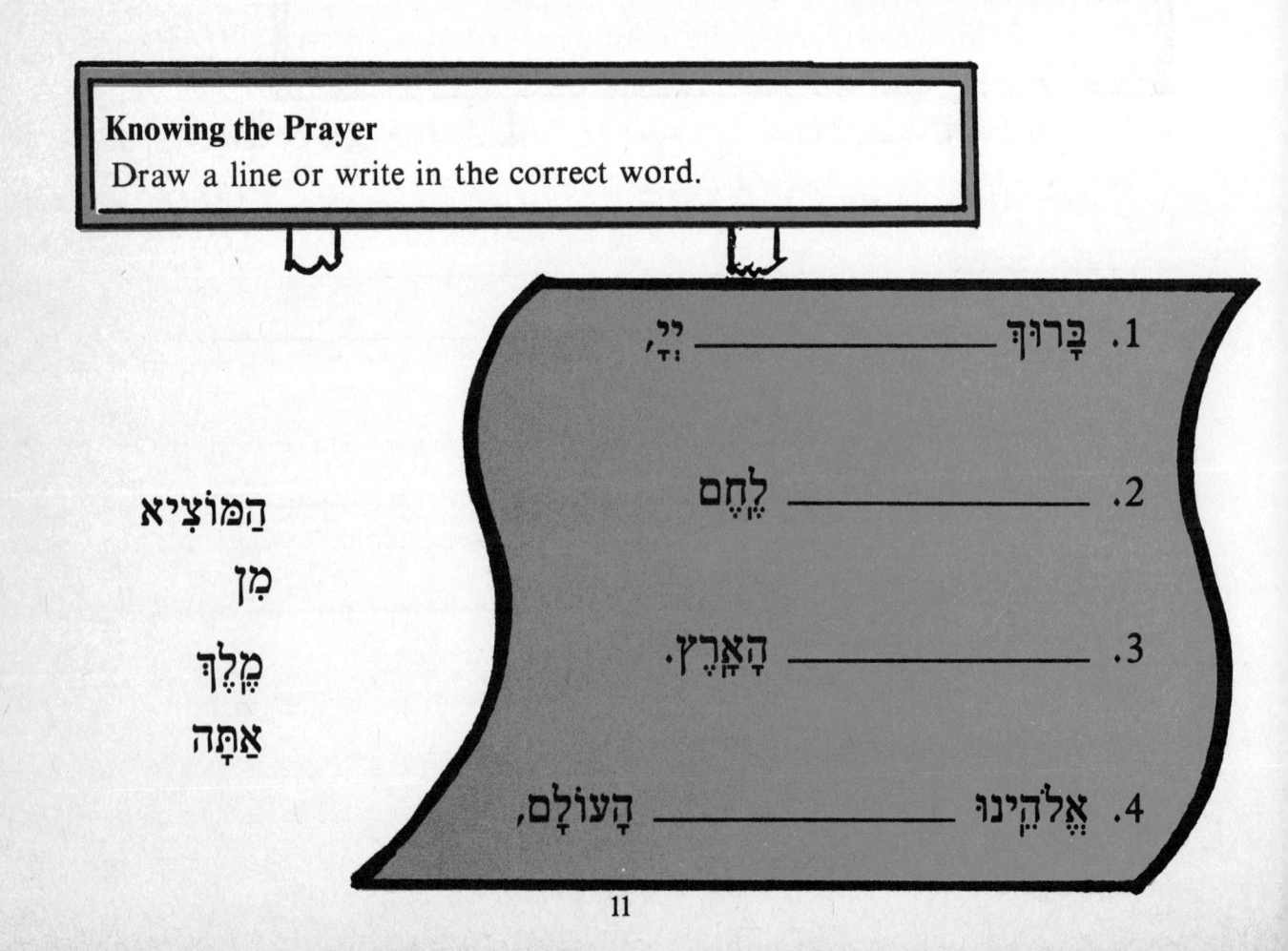

בָּרוּךְ אַתָּה יְיָ, אֱלֹהֵינוּ מֶלֶךְ הָעוֹלָם,
הַמּוֹצִיא לֶחֶם מִן הָאָרֶץ.

Knowing the Prayer
Draw a line or write in the correct word.

1. בָּרוּךְ _____ יְיָ,

2. _____ לֶחֶם

3. הָאָרֶץ. _____

4. אֱלֹהֵינוּ _____ הָעוֹלָם,

הַמּוֹצִיא
מִן
מֶלֶךְ
אַתָּה

Knowing the Ideas
Draw a line from the Hebrew phrase to the correct idea.

1. God is.   הַמּוֹצִיא לֶחֶם מִן הָאָרֶץ
2. God feeds the world.   בָּרוּךְ אַתָּה יְיָ
3. We thank God.   אֱלֹהֵינוּ מֶלֶךְ הָעוֹלָם

Knowing the Answers
Write your answer to each of the questions.

1. Why is God compared to a king?
_____
_____

2. Does God really bring forth bread from the earth?
_____
_____

3. Who raises wheat and corn and all kinds of vegetables?
_____
_____

4. Why do we praise God for bringing forth bread from the earth?
_____
_____

Knowing the Prefixes
Fill in the missing translations.

1. מֶלֶךְ means king   הַמֶּלֶךְ means the king
2. לֶחֶם means _____   הַלֶּחֶם means _____
3. אֶרֶץ means _____   הָאָרֶץ means _____
4. עוֹלָם means _____   הָעוֹלָם means _____

The prefix הָ or הַ before a noun means _____

The מֶלֶךְ and the Farmer

The אֶרֶץ of Gimpel was ruled by a wise מֶלֶךְ. One day הַמֶּלֶךְ was riding his horse. הַמֶּלֶךְ saw a farmer working in הָאָרֶץ.

הַמֶּלֶךְ asked the farmer, "What are אַתָּה planting in הָאָרֶץ?"

The farmer replied, "I am planting wheat in הָאָרֶץ."

"What will אַתָּה do with the wheat after it is harvested?" asked הַמֶּלֶךְ.

"I," replied the farmer, "will bake the wheat into לֶחֶם. The לֶחֶם will feed the people in your אֶרֶץ."

הַמֶּלֶךְ smiled and said, "I and my people thank אַתָּה for bringing forth לֶחֶם מִן הָאָרֶץ."

The farmer looked into the eyes of הַמֶּלֶךְ and replied, "Do not thank me. Thank אֱלֹהֵינוּ מֶלֶךְ הָעוֹלָם, הַמּוֹצִיא לֶחֶם מִן הָאָרֶץ."

The Miracle of Creation

It's fun to play and swim in the sun. But the sun gives us much, much more than fun. From the sun comes something that not a single person, plant, or animal on earth could do without—that thing is called energy. It is energy that makes us walk, talk, run, and do all the things we are able to do. Much of the energy humans and animals receive from the sun comes through their food. The sun shines on seeds in the earth, and fills them with energy. That is the first link in the chain. The seeds pass the energy along to the plants, and that is the next link. People and animals eat the plants and get the energy they need for life. Human beings also get energy by eating the animals which have eaten the plants.

We call this kind of food chain an "eco system." It is only one very tiny part of all the other systems God created. Later on, in high school, you will study many of these other systems and learn much more about them. Even the greatest scientists in the world are still studying these systems. They are learning more each day about how all the parts fit together and depend on each other. They are also learning that we must treat these wonderful systems of life with great care so that they will not be destroyed.

The eco system makes us see what great miracles all of God's creations are. As human beings, we could study these wonders for a million years and we would still be unable to create a single miracle.

What Do You Think?

1. Your yard or porch is an eco system. What is the first link? What is the second link? Where does the chain end?
2. Name some food chains.
3. How does the food chain of a chicken work? A fish? A cow?
4. How does your food chain work?
5. Which food chain is longer? Yours or that of an ant?

בִּרְכַּת הַמָּזוֹן
Grace After Meals

Knowing the Prayer Vocabulary

וּבְרַחֲמִים	and with mercy	הַזָּן	who feeds
נוֹתֵן	gives	כֻּלוֹ	the whole world
לֶחֶם	bread	כָּל	all
כָּל־בָּשָׂר	all living things	בְּטוּבוֹ	with His goodness
בָּשָׂר	living things, meat	טוֹב	good
חַסְדוֹ	His kindness	בְּחֵן	with grace
חֶסֶד	kindness	בְּחֶסֶד	with kindness

Knowing the Words
Circle the correct Hebrew word.

1. who feeds	בְּטוּבוֹ	כֻּלּוֹ	הַזָּן
2. with His goodness	בְּטוּבוֹ	אַתָּה	בָּרוּךְ
3. with grace	וּבְרַחֲמִים	בְּחֶסֶד	בְּחֵן
4. with kindness	בְּחֶסֶד	מֶלֶךְ	אֱלֹהֵינוּ
5. and with mercy	הָעוֹלָם כֻּלּוֹ	וּבְרַחֲמִים	הַזָּן
6. kindness	חֶסֶד	כִּי	הוּא
7. grace	נוֹתֵן	לְעוֹלָם	טוֹב
8. mercy	לֶחֶם	רַחֲמִים	הוּא
9. bread	חַסְדּוֹ	לֶחֶם	חֵן
10. all living things	הַזָּן	בָּרוּךְ	כָּל־בָּשָׂר
11. His kindness	לְכָל־בָּשָׂר	אֶת־הָעוֹלָם	חַסְדּוֹ

אָמֵן, so much a part of our religious services, is found only twelve times in the Bible.

Before we eat or drink, we say a blessing to thank God for giving us food. After we eat or drink, we recite בִּרְכַּת הַמָּזוֹן, the Grace After Meals, which is made up of beautiful prayers of thanksgiving.

We say the Grace After Meals to remind us that even when we are filled with food and are satisfied, we must be just as thankful to God as we were when we were hungry and had just begun to eat.

Blessed are You, Eternal,	בָּרוּךְ אַתָּה יְיָ,
our God, ruler of the world,	אֱלֹהֵינוּ מֶלֶךְ הָעוֹלָם,
who feeds the whole world	הַזָּן אֶת־הָעוֹלָם כֻּלּוֹ
with His (God's) goodness, with grace,	בְּטוּבוֹ, בְּחֵן,
with kindness, and with mercy	בְּחֶסֶד וּבְרַחֲמִים,
He (God) gives bread	הוּא נוֹתֵן לֶחֶם
to all living things	לְכָל־בָּשָׂר,
because His (God's) kindness is forever.	כִּי לְעוֹלָם חַסְדּוֹ.
Blessed are You, Eternal,	בָּרוּךְ אַתָּה יְיָ,
who feeds all living things.	הַזָּן אֶת־הַכֹּל.

Knowing the Phrases
Draw a line from the Hebrew phrase to its English meaning.

---

1. who feeds all living things   הַזָּן אֶת־הַכֹּל
2. because God's kindness is forever   הַזָּן אֶת־הָעוֹלָם כֻּלּוֹ
3. who feeds all living things   בְּחֶסֶד וּבְרַחֲמִים
4. with kindness, and with mercy   כִּי לְעוֹלָם חַסְדּוֹ

The בִּרְכַּת הַמָּזוֹן praises God, הַזָּן אֶת־הָעוֹלָם כֻּלּוֹ בְּטוּבוֹ. We acknowledge the foods that grow as gifts from God.

בָּרוּךְ אַתָּה יְיָ, אֱלֹהֵינוּ מֶלֶךְ הָעוֹלָם, הַזָּן אֶת הָעוֹלָם כֻּלּוֹ בְּטוּבוֹ; בְּחֵן בְּחֶסֶד וּבְרַחֲמִים, הוּא נוֹתֵן לֶחֶם לְכָל בָּשָׂר, כִּי לְעוֹלָם חַסְדּוֹ.

בָּרוּךְ אַתָּה יְיָ, הַזָּן אֶת הַכֹּל.

Knowing the Answers
Write your answer to each of the questions.

1. Who is the "our" in "our God"?

2. Why do we recite blessings before and after a meal?

Knowing the Prefixes
Fill in the missing translations.

1. חֵן means grace   בְּחֵן means with grace
2. חֶסֶד means _____   בְּחֶסֶד means _____
3. רַחֲמִים means _____   בְּרַחֲמִים means _____
4. טוּבוֹ means _____   בְּטוּבוֹ means _____
5. חַסְדוֹ means _____   בְּחַסְדוֹ means _____

The prefix בְּ or בְ in front of a word means _____

Knowing the Prayer
Draw a line or write in the correct word.

בְּחֵן
לֶחֶם
כֻּלוֹ
חַסְדוֹ

1. הַזָּן אֶת־הָעוֹלָם _____ בְּטוּבוֹ
2. הוּא נוֹתֵן _____ לְכָל־בָּשָׂר
3. _____ בְּחֶסֶד וּבְרַחֲמִים
4. כִּי לְעוֹלָם _____

Laws For the Needy

In the בִּרְכַּת הַמָּזוֹן prayer we thank God, who provides food for all living things.

We show our appreciation for God's חֵן, חֶסֶד, and רַחֲמִים by sharing with others who are in need. We give צְדָקָה and support institutions which help poor and sick people.

No people of old showed as much concern shown for the livelihood of those in want as in Israel. In the ancient Hebrew state, the poor were assured of a living by their rights which the Bible gave them in the harvest. These rights were five in number:

1. The poor had the right to any crops that grew in the corners of the field—פֵּאָה ("corner").

2. The poor had the right to crops dropped on the ground when the corn was being picked—לֶקֶט ("gathering").

3. The poor had the right to grapes that were dropped in the vineyard—פֶּרֶט ("dropping").

4. The poor had the right to grapes that were not perfect—עוֹלְלוֹת ("young clusters").

5. The poor had the right to crops that were forgotten by the farmer—שִׁכְחָה ("forgetfulness").

All these parts of the harvest belonged to the poor. The farmer was not allowed to gather them, and all needy people—the poor, the widow, the orphan, and the stranger (whether Jew or non-Jew)—were entitled to them.

There was also a special poor tax, known as מַעֲשֵׂר עָנִי, "Poor Tithe." Every third year, the Jewish farmer had to set aside one-tenth of his harvest and take it to a special storehouse in his district where the מַעֲשֵׂר עָנִי was kept for distributing to the needy, even outside from אֶרֶץ יִשְׂרָאֵל, some Jews continued to give one-tenth of their earnings (tithe) מַעֲשֵׂר to צְדָקָה.

Whom Will You Support?

Suppose that when you become an adult, you decide to "מַעֲשֵׂר" your earnings. How would you distribute your money?

Look at this community map. Decide which three places will receive your support. Tell why you would contribute to those institutions.

I would support the _____ because _____.

I would support the _____ because _____.

I would support the _____ because _____.

בִּרְכַּת הַנֵּרוֹת לְשַׁבָּת
Shabbat Candle-Lighting

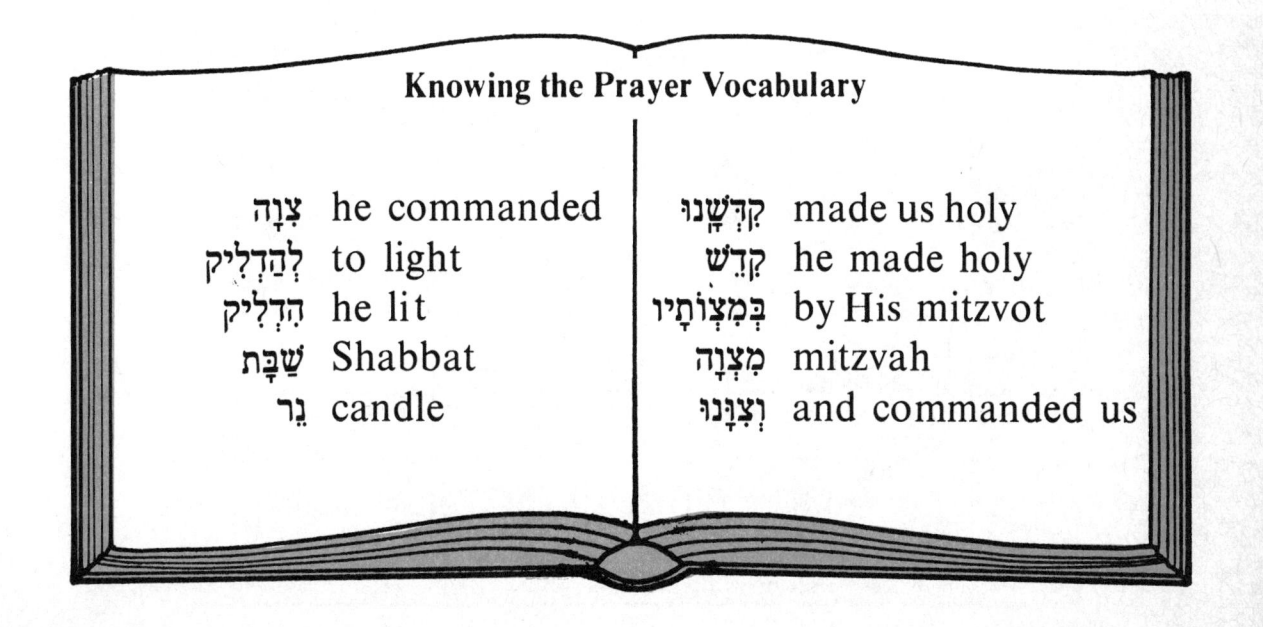

Knowing the Prayer Vocabulary

צִוָּה	he commanded	קִדְּשָׁנוּ	made us holy
לְהַדְלִיק	to light	קִדֵּשׁ	he made holy
הִדְלִיק	he lit	בְּמִצְוֹתָיו	by His mitzvot
שַׁבָּת	Shabbat	מִצְוָה	mitzvah
נֵר	candle	וְצִוָּנוּ	and commanded us

Knowing the Words
Circle the correct Hebrew word.

1. candle	נֵר	בָּרוּךְ	אֱלֹהֵינוּ	
2. to light	הָעוֹלָם	לְהַדְלִיק	וְצִוָּנוּ	
3. made us holy	קִדְּשָׁנוּ	אַתָּה	יְיָ	
4. by His mitzvot	אֲשֶׁר	יְיָ	בְּמִצְוֹתָיו	
5. mitzvah	מִצְוָה	מֶלֶךְ	אַתָּה	
6. and commanded us	וְצִוָּנוּ	בְּמִצְוֹתָיו	אֱלֹהֵינוּ	
7. of Shabbat	שֶׁל־שַׁבָּת	נֵר	מֶלֶךְ	

In ancient Israel, six blasts were blown with a trumpet on Friday before sunset. The third blast meant that it was time to light the Shabbat candles.

Just as creation began with the joyous words "Let there be light," so does the Sabbath begin with light. We welcome the Shabbat by performing the מִצְוָה of lighting the Shabbat candles. The brightly burning candles create an atmosphere of harmony, love, peace, and family togetherness.

Blessed are You, Eternal,	בָּרוּךְ אַתָּה יְיָ,
our God, ruler of the world	אֱלֹהֵינוּ מֶלֶךְ הָעוֹלָם,
who made us holy	אֲשֶׁר קִדְּשָׁנוּ
by His (God's) mitzvot	בְּמִצְוֹתָיו,
and commanded us to light	וְצִוָּנוּ לְהַדְלִיק
the candle(s) of Shabbat.	נֵר שֶׁל-שַׁבָּת.

Knowing the Phrases
Draw a line from the Hebrew phrase to its English meaning.

1. who made us holy by His mitzvot — בָּרוּךְ אַתָּה יְיָ
2. to light the candle of Shabbat — אֱלֹהֵינוּ מֶלֶךְ הָעוֹלָם
3. Blessed are You, Eternal — אֲשֶׁר קִדְּשָׁנוּ בְּמִצְוֹתָיו
4. our God, ruler of the world — לְהַדְלִיק נֵר שֶׁל-שַׁבָּת

It is customary to add a silent prayer for peace and the health and the welfare of friends and family.

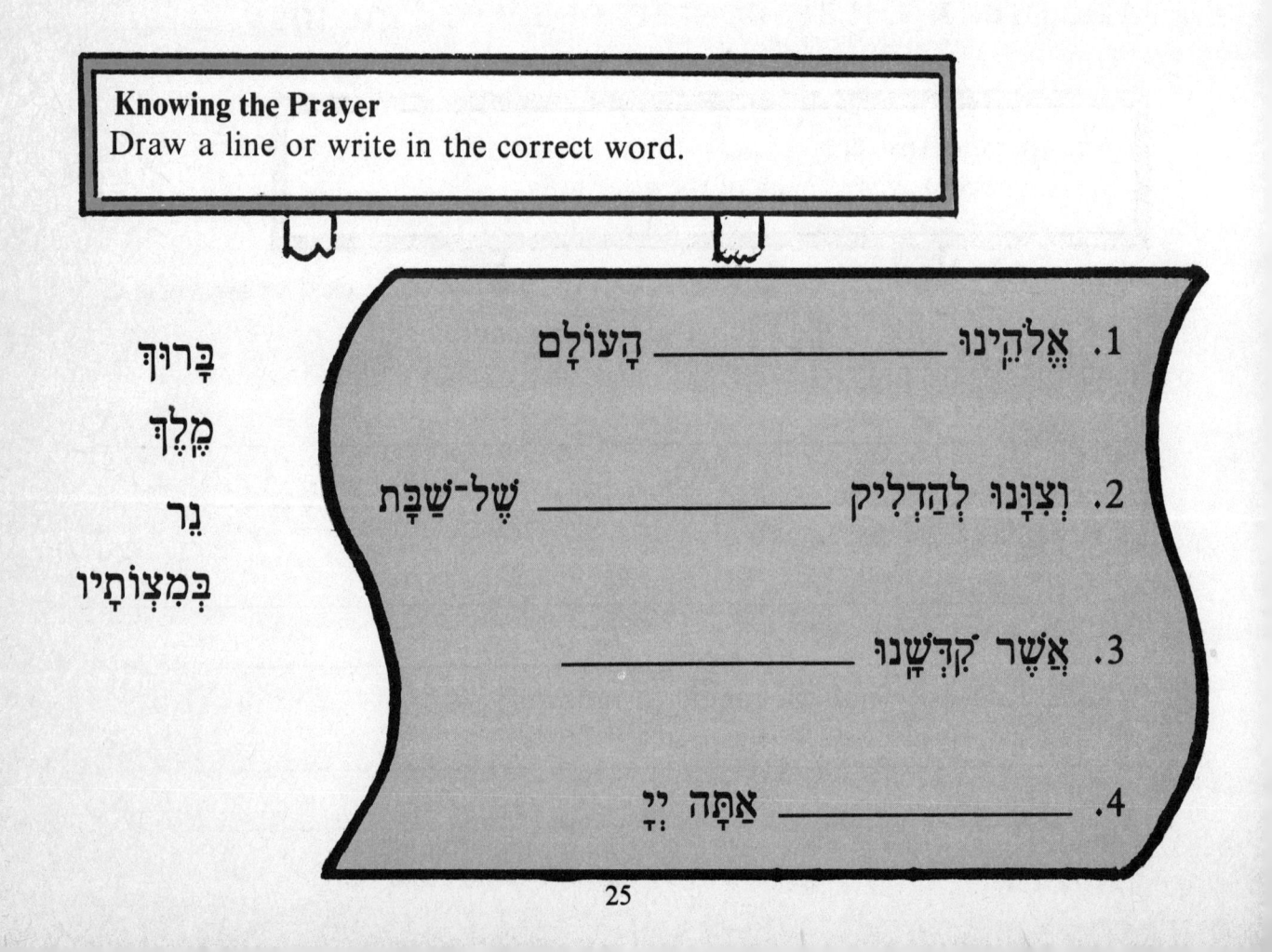

בָּרוּךְ אַתָּה יְיָ, אֱלֹהֵינוּ מֶלֶךְ הָעוֹלָם, אֲשֶׁר קִדְּשָׁנוּ בְּמִצְוֹתָיו, וְצִוָּנוּ לְהַדְלִיק נֵר שֶׁל־שַׁבָּת.

Knowing the Prayer
Draw a line or write in the correct word.

1. אֱלֹהֵינוּ _____ הָעוֹלָם

2. וְצִוָּנוּ לְהַדְלִיק _____ שֶׁל־שַׁבָּת

3. אֲשֶׁר קִדְּשָׁנוּ _____

4. _____ אַתָּה יְיָ

בָּרוּךְ
מֶלֶךְ
נֵר
בְּמִצְוֹתָיו

Knowing the Prefixes
Fill in the missing translations.

1. כַּלָּה means bride   הַכַּלָּה means the bride

2. נֵר means _____   הַנֵר means _____

3. שַׁבָּת means _____   הַשַׁבָּת means _____

The prefix הַ, הָ at the start of a word means _____

Knowing the Answers
Write your answer to each of the questions.

1. What six words in the Sabbath Hebrew candle-lighting prayer are the same as in the *Motzi* prayer?
_____
_____

2. How has God made us holy?
_____
_____

3. Is lighting the Sabbath candles a mitzvah?
_____
_____

מִצְווֹת
Mitzvot

Did you ever wonder when the great Jewish laws were written down? Not just a few years ago, but 3,000 years ago.

In those days, hardly anyone cared about what happened to people when they got sick or grew old or were poor. There was no such thing as welfare for people who were unable to work. There were no comfortable homes for old people where they could be cared for. Today, when people grow old, the government pays them social security. But 3,000 years ago, there was nothing like that. There were no unions and only a very few courts of justice. There weren't even any hospitals—imagine that!

But even in those long-ago times, the Jews cared very deeply about their people who were old, sick or helpless. So they followed rules for living so that people would be protected and justice would be done. Our rabbis teach us that these rules are called מִצְווֹת.

There are 613 of these rules, or *mitzvot,* and there are two different kinds. One kind is called YES, DO *mitzvot,* and the other is called NO, DO NOT *mitzvot.*

There are 248 YES, DO *mitzvot.* "YES, DO *mitzvot*" are called in Hebrew מִצְווֹת עֲשֵׂה.

If we want to live in a holy way, then we must do God's will by observing מִצְווֹת. At the same time that we do God's will, we also help ourselves, because a מִצְוָה can make us happier or healthier or wiser or just better people.

There are 613 מִצְווֹת in our Torah. There are מִצְווֹת about holidays and ceremonies and many מִצְווֹת about how to treat other people—like honoring your parents, sharing with others, helping people, being honest. When we do these מִצְווֹת, we are doing something God wants us to do. Then we are good and we *feel good* too.

It is a מִצְוָה to pray. You know how it helps just to talk things over with your parents or friends. It helps even more to talk to God. Prayer is a *mitzvah* that makes us feel better inside ourselves.

You might not know it, but study is a מִצְוָה too, and a very important one. Parents and teachers used to give children honey cakes or drops of honey on the day their studies began. This showed the children that the study of the Torah is sweet and encouraged them to learn. Study is so important because it helps us to learn God's will. When we study the Torah, we learn about more מִצְווֹת that we can do.

One מִצְוָה leads to another. For example, when you help someone, you may feel so good inside that before you know it, you find yourself helping someone else! Or when your family has a Passover סֶדֶר, they may also do the מִצְוָה of inviting a guest to share the holiday with them.

The more *mitzvot* you do, the more you follow God's will, and you will be happier for it.

There are 365 NO, DO NOT *mitzvot*. In Hebrew these are called מִצְווֹת לֹא־תַעֲשֶׂה. One of these is: NO, DO NOT STEAL. What do you think some of the others might be?

_____

_____

What Do You Think?

1. What is a מִצְוָה?
2. Why is it important to do מִצְווֹת?
3. Can you think of a מִצְוָה that you did recently? How did you feel when you did it?
4. Do you think it's important to do a מִצְוָה willingly and wholeheartedly?
5. What if you did the מִצְוָה of giving צְדָקָה, but you really didn't feel like doing it? Would it be better than not giving צְדָקָה at all?

It's a Mitzvah to Share

Let's follow some mitzvot through a chain.
Try to think of ways in which the following mitzvah might lead to other mitzvot.

Situation One:
You are playing in the street, suddenly you see someone who seems sick.
You run over and help the person.
What other mitzvot may this lead to in the future?

_____

_____

_____

Situation Two:
A foreign student is in your class. She is having trouble with her schoolwork. You offer to help her after school.
What other mitzvot may result from this one mitzvah?

_____

_____

There was a special room in the Temple in יְרוּשָׁלַיִם. In this room, the rich people would leave money for the poor to take so that neither was seen by the other.
In this way, the poor could receive צְדָקָה with dignity.

קִדּוּשׁ
Kiddush

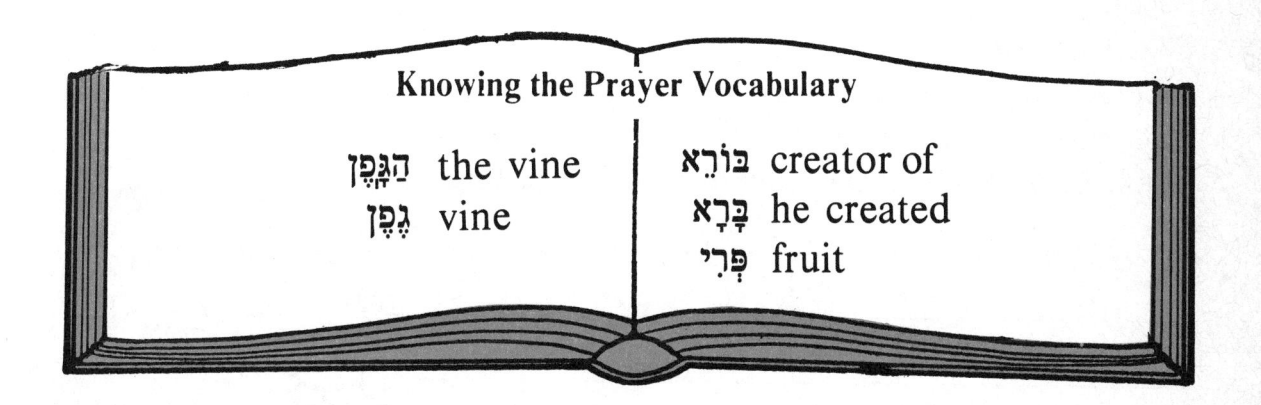

Knowing the Prayer Vocabulary

הַגֶּפֶן the vine
גֶּפֶן vine

בּוֹרֵא creator of
בָּרָא he created
פְּרִי fruit

Knowing the Words
Circle the correct Hebrew word.

1. vine	בָּרוּךְ	הָעוֹלָם	גֶּפֶן
2. creator of	בָּרוּךְ	בּוֹרֵא	אַתָּה
3. the vine	הַגֶּפֶן	פְּרִי	מֶלֶךְ
4. fruit	מֶלֶךְ	פְּרִי	הָעוֹלָם
5. he created	אַתָּה	אֱלֹהֵינוּ	בָּרָא

"And God blessed the seventh day, declaring it holy . . ." We, too, bring in the שַׁבָּת by declaring it holy, with the קִדּוּשׁ prayer recited over a cup of wine. So begins the שַׁבָּת meal on Friday evening. When Mother has lit the שַׁבָּת candles, and the table is beautifully set, with two חַלוֹת covered by a cloth, the family gathers around the table, ready to welcome the Sabbath Queen. You hold the cup of wine and chant קִדּוּשׁ. Then all respond אָמֵן and drink the wine.

Blessed are You, Eternal, בָּרוּךְ אַתָּה יְיָ,
    our God, ruler of the world, אֱלֹהֵינוּ מֶלֶךְ הָעוֹלָם,
    creator of the fruit of the vine. בּוֹרֵא פְּרִי הַגָּפֶן.

Knowing the Phrases
Draw a line from the Hebrew phrase to its English meaning.

1. Blessed are You, Eternal   בּוֹרֵא פְּרִי הַגָּפֶן
2. our God, ruler of the world   אֱלֹהֵינוּ מֶלֶךְ הָעוֹלָם
3. creator of the fruit of the vine   בָּרוּךְ אַתָּה יְיָ

The קִדּוּשׁ retells the story of how God created the world in six days and rested on the seventh, blessing that day and declaring it holy. It reminds us why we celebrate שַׁבָּת and how lucky we are that we are free to observe it.

$$\text{בָּרוּךְ אַתָּה יְיָ, אֱלֹהֵינוּ מֶלֶךְ הָעוֹלָם,}$$
$$\text{בּוֹרֵא פְּרִי הַגָּפֶן.}$$

See page 153 for the complete קִדּוּשׁ

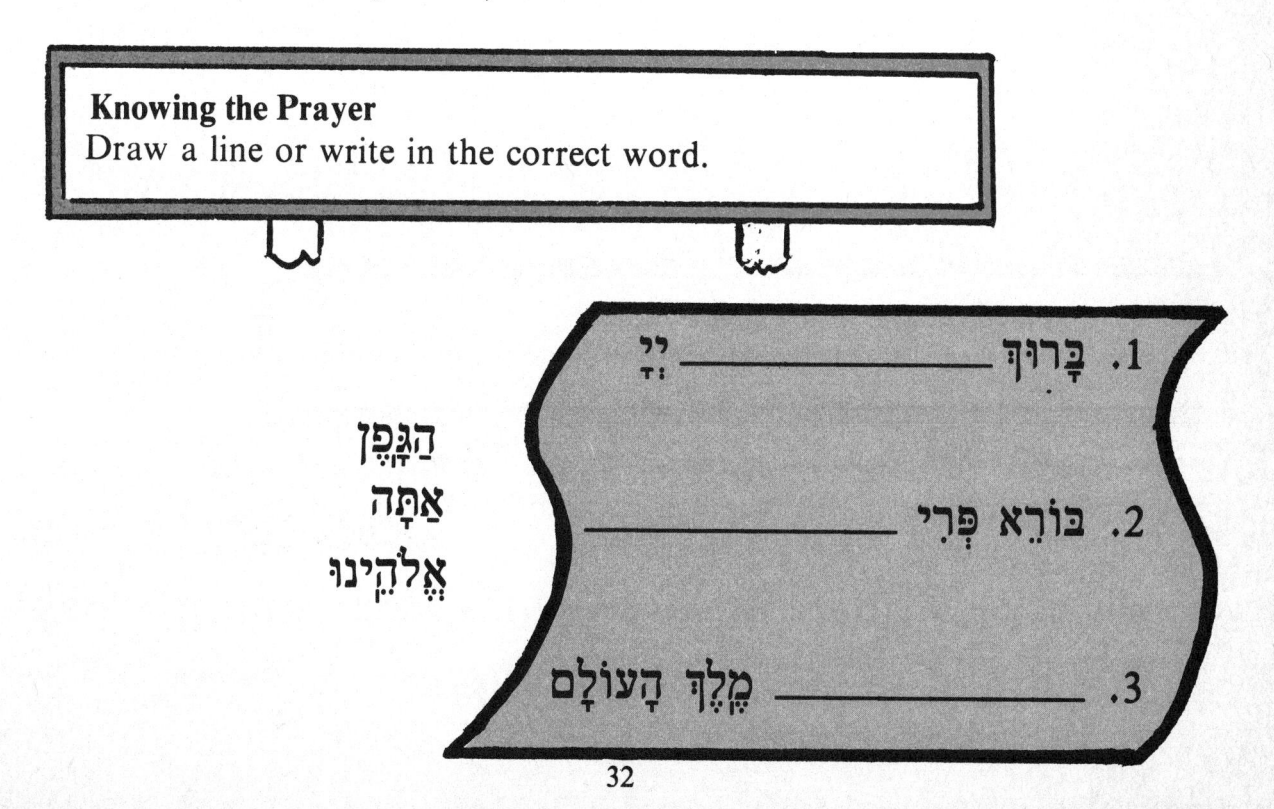

Knowing the Prayer
Draw a line or write in the correct word.

הַגָּפֶן
אַתָּה
אֱלֹהֵינוּ

1. בָּרוּךְ _____ יְיָ

2. בּוֹרֵא פְּרִי _____

3. _____ מֶלֶךְ הָעוֹלָם

Knowing the Prefixes
Fill in the missing words.

1. עוֹלָם means world   הָעוֹלָם means the world
2. מֶלֶךְ means _____   הַמֶּלֶךְ means _____
3. גֶּפֶן means _____   הַגֶּפֶן means _____
4. פְּרִי means _____   הַפְּרִי means _____

The prefix הָ or הַ before a word means _____.

The first printed prayer book was published by Soncino in 1486. By the end of the seventeenth century many printers' errors had crept into the Siddur. Segilman Baer, a European scholar, re-edited the Siddur on the basis of old manuscripts and in 1868 gave the world the famous Baer Siddur. It is one of the most scholarly Siddurim ever published.

הַשַּׁבָּת
The Sabbath

"אָמֵן. בָּרוּךְ. חַלָּה." Two-year-old David pointed excitedly at the table, all set for the Sabbath with gleaming china and silver, candles burning brightly, חַלּוֹת under the special *challah* cover, silver wine cup, and wine. Everything was ready for Father's return from synagogue. David made a dive for the חַלָּה.

"No, no, David," Mother stopped him gently. "Daddy will be home soon. He'll make קִדּוּשׁ first and then . . ." At the word קִדּוּשׁ, David ran to the bookshelf and grabbed a סִדּוּר. Returning to the dining room, he took his cup from the highchair, opened the סִדּוּר, and said, "בָּרוּךְ. אָמֵן." He smiled proudly.

"Very good, David," said Mother, giving him a hug.

Miriam stood in the doorway, lost in thought. Mechanically she folded and unfolded her arms. "Mom," she said suddenly, "why is David always so excited about the Sabbath? I mean, what can he understand about it? He's only a baby."

"Well, I guess he picks up things from us. And, anyway, who's to say that he doesn't have a נְשָׁמָה יְתֵרָה too?"

"A what?"

"A different soul, a special Sabbath spirit. You know what I mean?"

"Well, it does feel different around here on the Sabbath; that's true. The meal is special; there's קִדּוּשׁ, the blessing over the חַלָּה, the Sabbath songs we sing. . . David gets to go to synagogue with all of us. And there's הַבְדָּלָה at the end of the Sabbath, too."

"And not only that. When I think about it, on the Sabbath we're together more as a family. It's when we have our best talks. Like this one."

Miriam smiled. Mother smiled. And David happily proclaimed "שַׁבָּת."

"And God blessed the seventh day, declaring it holy..." We, too, bring in the Sabbath by declaring it holy, with the קִדּוּשׁ prayer recited over a cup of wine. So begins the Sabbath meal on Friday evening. When Mother has lit the Sabbath candles, and the table is beautifully set, with two *challot* covered by a cloth, the family gathers around the table ready to welcome the Sabbath Queen. Father and you too hold the cup of wine and chant the קִדּוּשׁ. Then all respond אָמֵן and drink the wine.

The קִדּוּשׁ prayer retells the story of how God created the world in six days and rested on the seventh, blessing that day and declaring it holy. It reminds us why we celebrate the Sabbath and how lucky we are that we are free to observe it.

Shabbat Shalom

On Shabbat we greet each other with the words *Shabbat Shalom,* "A Peaceful Sabbath!" What makes Shabbat a more peaceful day than other days of the week? Try to think of at least three things.

1. _____

2. _____

3. _____

לְכָה דוֹדִי
Come My Beloved

Knowing the Prayer Vocabulary

פְּנֵי	presence (the face of)	לְכָה	come
פָּנִים	face	הָלַךְ	he went
נְקַבְּלָה	let us greet	דוֹדִי	my beloved
קִבֵּל	he greeted, received	לִקְרַאת	towards
		כַּלָּה	bride

Knowing the Words
Circle the correct Hebrew word.

1. come	פְּנֵי	שַׁבָּת	לְכָה	
2. went	הָלַךְ	לְכָה	דוֹדִי	
3. my beloved	נְקַבְּלָה	דוֹדִי	כַּלָּה	
4. bride	שַׁבָּת	לִקְרַאת	כַּלָּה	
5. towards	יָד	לִקְרַאת	נְקַבְּלָה	
6. presence (the face of)	שַׁבָּת	נְקַבְּלָה	פְּנֵי	

36

This פִּיוּט (religious poem) was composed about 1540 by Rabbi Solomon Halevy Alkabetz, a scholar who lived in אֶרֶץ יִשְׂרָאֵל. He based it on the Talmudic passage, "Rabbi Haninah said, 'Let us go forth to greet the Sabbath Queen.' Rabbi Yannai said, 'Come, O bride! Come, O bride!'"

The author signed his name to the פִּיוּט in a Hebrew acrostic. Each verse, after the introductory first stanza or verse, except for the last verse, begins with a letter of the author's name: שָׁמוֹר, לִקְרַאת, מְקַדֵּשׁ, הִתְנַעֲרִי, הִתְעוֹרְרִי, לֹא וְהָיוּ, יָמִין. These letters form the name שְׁלֹמֹה הַלֵּוִי, Solomon the Levite.

Come, my beloved	לְכָה דוֹדִי
towards (to meet) the bride.	לִקְרַאת כַּלָּה.
The Shabbat presence,	פְּנֵי שַׁבָּת
let us greet.	נְקַבְּלָה.

Knowing the Phrases
Draw a line from the Hebrew phrase to its English meaning.

1. The Shabbat presence, let us greet   לְכָה דוֹדִי לִקְרַאת כַּלָּה

2. Come, my beloved, to meet the bride   פְּנֵי שַׁבָּת נְקַבְּלָה

As we say the last verse of the לְכָה דוֹדִי, we rise and face the entrance of the synagogue as a sign that we are welcoming Shabbat.

It is a custom at this point in the service to welcome any mourners who have suffered a death in the family during the previous week.

לְכָה דוֹדִי לִקְרַאת כַּלָה. פְּנֵי שַׁבָּת נְקַבְּלָה: לְכָה דוֹדִי

See page 155 for the complete לְכָה דוֹדִי

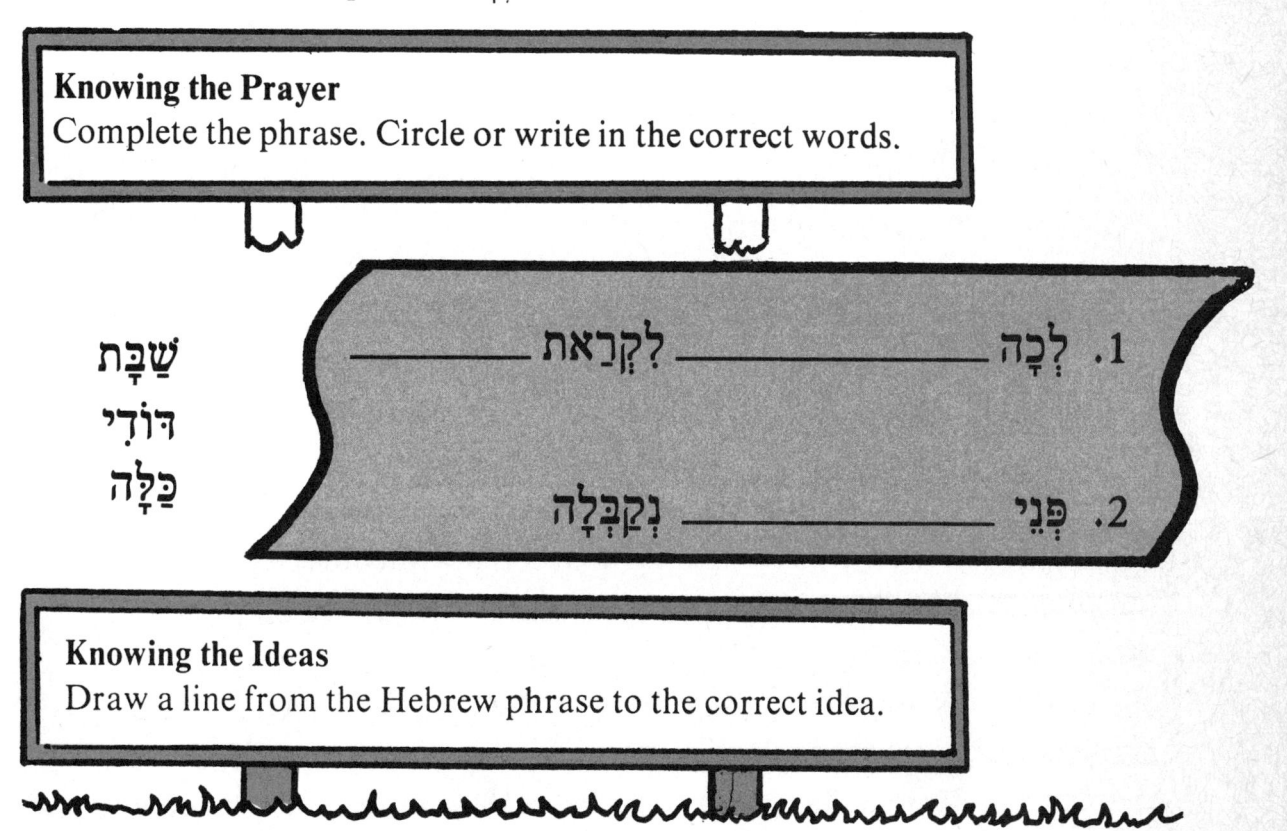

Knowing the Prayer
Complete the phrase. Circle or write in the correct words.

שַׁבָּת
דוֹדִי
כַּלָה

1. לְכָה _____ לִקְרַאת _____

2. פְּנֵי _____ נְקַבְּלָה

Knowing the Ideas
Draw a line from the Hebrew phrase to the correct idea.

1. The Shabbat is compared to a bride   פְּנֵי שַׁבָּת נְקַבְּלָה

2. Jews welcome the Shabbat with joy.   לְכָה דוֹדִי לִקְרַאת כַּלָה

The Rabbi

The authority in Jewish religious life is the רַבִּי. The rabbbis earn their position because they have studied and mastered Jewish law. Their knowledge entitles them to this special privilege of giving decisions on questions of Jewish law.

Today, rabbis are the spiritual leaders of congregations. They preach sermons, conduct services, officiate at weddings and the funerals, visit the sick and comfort those who have had a death in the family.

The title רַבִּי is almost two thousand years old. In those days, scholars who have studied under the scholars of אֶרֶץ יִשְׂרָאֵל were given the title רַבִּי. The title was conferred upon them in a ceremony called *Semichah*.

The master would place his hands on the shoulder of the pupil and would testify to the pupil's scholarship. The act served to demonstrate the passing on of the master's authority to the pupil.

In America, there are three great rabbinic seminaries. Orthodox rabbis study at and receive their Semichah from the Rabbi Isaac Elchanan Theological Seminary of Yeshiva University. The Jewish Theological Seminary of America trains rabbis to serve the Conservative Movement. Hebrew Union College-Jewish Institute of Religion, trains rabbis for service in reform congregations.

The Happy Angel

There is a Midrash that tells of two angels that fly with every person that leaves the synagogue on Friday evening and wends his way homeward. One angel is a Good Angel, dressed in white, with a kind face and a sweet smile. The other is a Bad Angel. When they reach the house, the angels rush ahead and peek inside. If the house is not cleaned, if the candles are not lit, the table not set—in short, if the people who live there are not ready to meet the Sabbath Queen—the Bad Angel claps his hands in glee. "Ha!" he cries. "May all the Sabbaths of this family be like this one! So be it! So be it!" And the Good Angel, much as he dislikes to, must say "Amen."

But if there is a special Sabbath glow, and a spirit of warmth and expectation fills every nook and cranny of the house, the Bad Angel's scowl deepens and he slinks away, while the Good Angel laughs and flutters his wings, saying: "Ah! May all your Sabbaths be like this one, dear friends!" And the Bad Angel, grumpy though he is, is forced to say, "Amen!"

What Do You Think?

List all the ways you can think of to make Shabbat a special day.
Share your list with the class.

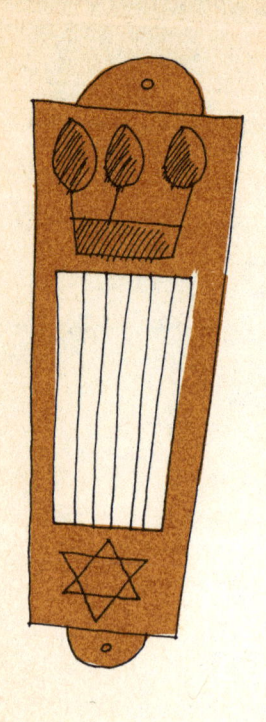

שְׁמַע
Shema

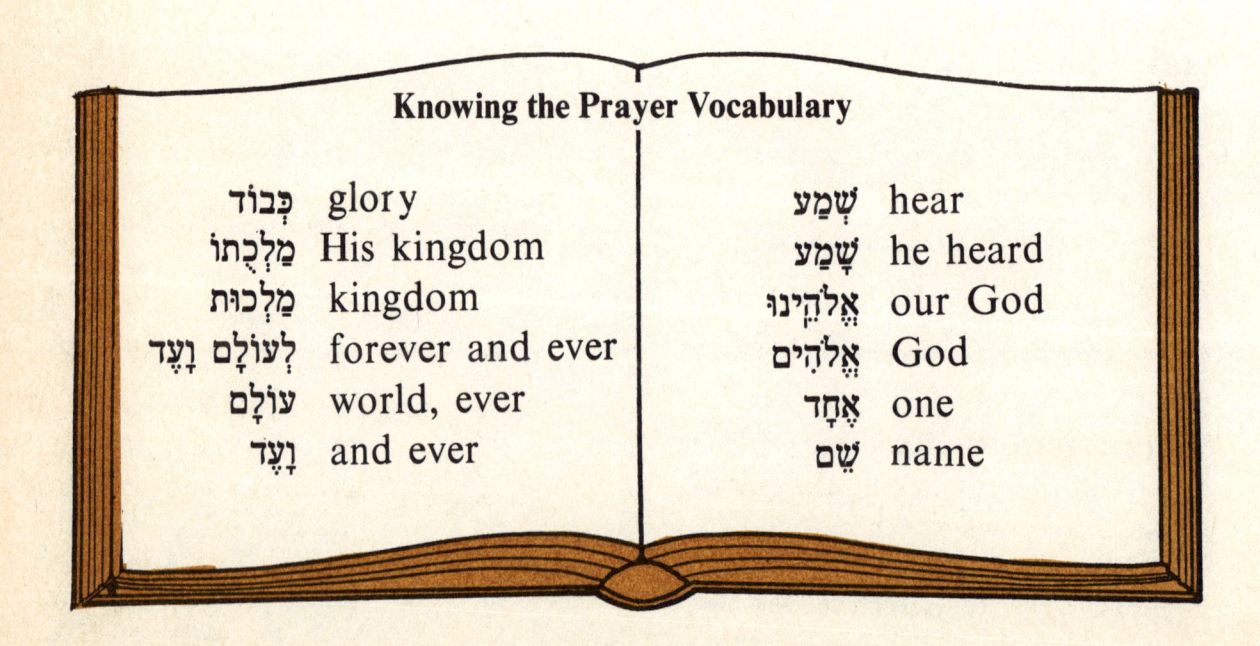

Knowing the Prayer Vocabulary

כָּבוֹד	glory	שְׁמַע	hear
מַלְכוּתוֹ	His kingdom	שָׁמַע	he heard
מַלְכוּת	kingdom	אֱלֹהֵינוּ	our God
לְעוֹלָם וָעֶד	forever and ever	אֱלֹהִים	God
עוֹלָם	world, ever	אֶחָד	one
וָעֶד	and ever	שֵׁם	name

Knowing the Words
Circle the correct Hebrew word.

1. hear	אֶחָד	יִשְׂרָאֵל	שְׁמַע	
2. Israel	הָאָרֶץ	יִשְׂרָאֵל	בָּרוּךְ	
3. one	אֶחָד	מָן	אֶחָד	
4. name	שֵׁם	הַגֶּפֶן	בּוֹרֵא	
5. God	פְּרִי	אֱלֹהִים	לֵב	
6. our God	אֱלֹהֵינוּ	בָּחַן	יְיָ	
7. glory	בְּחֶסֶד	לֶחֶם	כָּבוֹד	
8. His kingdom	הַמּוֹצִיא	מַלְכוּתוֹ	וּבְרַחֲמִים	
9. kingdom	מַלְכוּת	מֶלֶךְ	הָעוֹלָם	
10. is forever and ever	אֱלֹהֵינוּ	לְעוֹלָם וָעֶד	אַתָּה	

By the word יִשְׂרָאֵל, we mean the Children of Israel. You remember the story in the תּוֹרָה of how Jacob fought with the angel and his name was changed to Israel. All Jews are descended from Jacob. That is why we call ourselves the Children of Israel.

In the שְׁמַע we announce to all our people, to Israel, that there is a God and there is only one God. Then we pledge our love and devotion to God with every part of our beings. We promise to think about God throughout each day, to make God a part of us.

Hear, O Israel,	שְׁמַע יִשְׂרָאֵל,
the Eternal, is our God,	יְיָ אֱלֹהֵינוּ
the Eternal, is one.	יְיָ אֶחָד!
Blessed is the Name (of God),	בָּרוּךְ שֵׁם
the glory of His kingdom	כְּבוֹד מַלְכוּתוֹ
is forever and ever.	לְעוֹלָם וָעֶד.

Knowing the Phrases
Draw a line from the Hebrew phrase to its English meaning.

1. Hear, O Israel	לְעוֹלָם וָעֶד
2. the glory of His kingdom	שְׁמַע יִשְׂרָאֵל
3. the Eternal is One	יְיָ אֱלֹהֵינוּ
4. the Eternal is our God	יְיָ אֶחָד!
5. is forever and ever	כְּבוֹד מַלְכוּתוֹ

The prayer שְׁמַע contains our basic beliefs—the foundation of Judaism, the belief in one God and our devotion to God. It is therefor the most sacred of all our prayers—to be recited morning and night, שַׁחֲרִית, מַעֲרִיב.

שְׁמַע יִשְׂרָאֵל, יְיָ אֱלֹהֵינוּ, יְיָ אֶחָד!
בָּרוּךְ שֵׁם כְּבוֹד מַלְכוּתוֹ לְעוֹלָם וָעֶד.

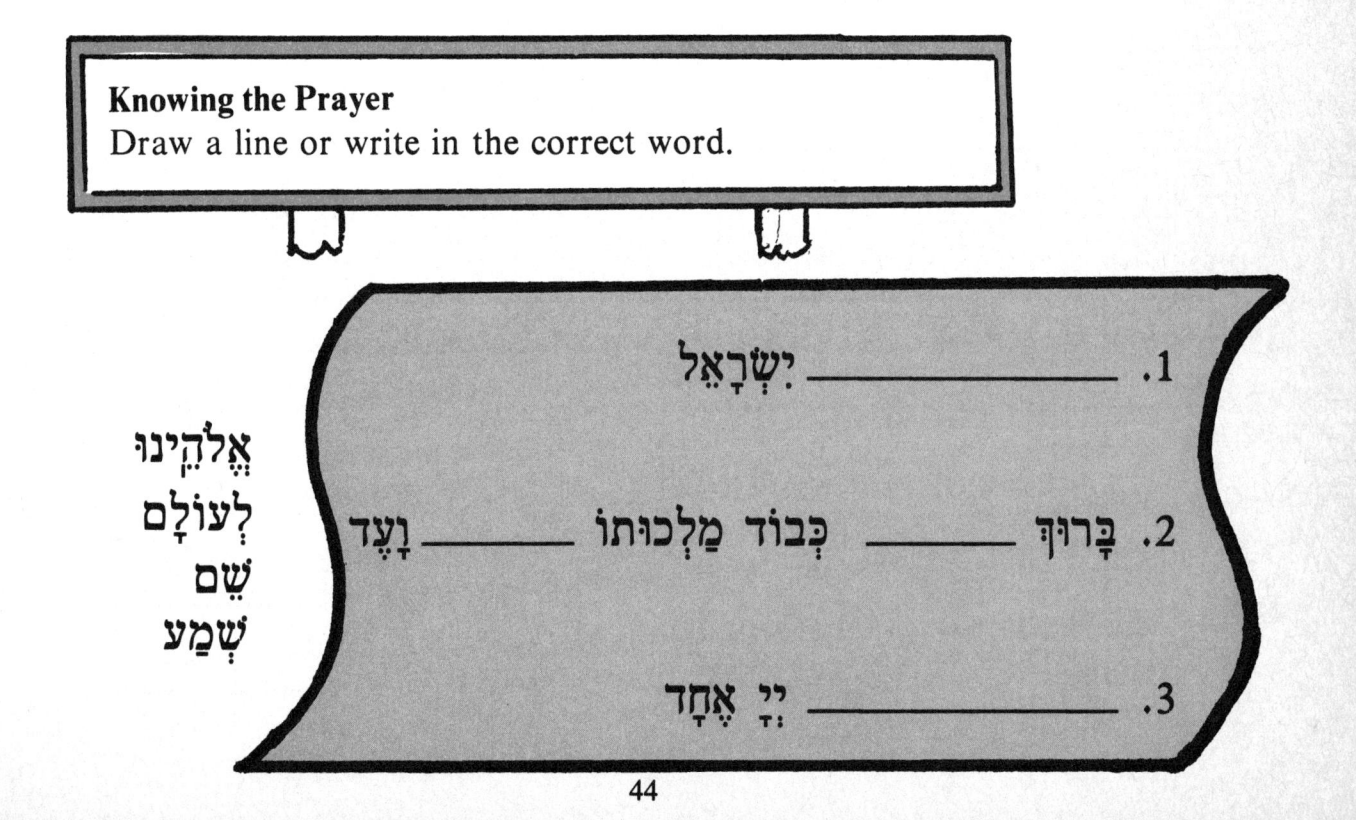

Knowing the Prayer
Draw a line or write in the correct word.

1. _____ יִשְׂרָאֵל

אֱלֹהֵינוּ
לְעוֹלָם
שֵׁם
שְׁמַע

2. בָּרוּךְ _____ כְּבוֹד מַלְכוּתוֹ _____ וָעֶד

3. _____ יְיָ אֶחָד

Knowing the Answers
Write your answer to each of the questions.

1. Who is One?
   _____
   _____

2. Can there be two and three?
   _____
   _____

3. Who is the King whose kingdom is forever?
   _____
   _____

Knowing the Suffixes
Fill in the missing words.

1. מַלְכוּת means kingdom   מַלְכוּתוֹ means His kingdom
2. לֶחֶם means _____   לַחְמוֹ means _____
3. אֶרֶץ means _____   אַרְצוֹ means _____
4. כָּבוֹד means _____   כְּבוֹדוֹ means _____

The suffix וֹ at the end of a word means _____

45

Discovering

In a world filled with idol worshippers and cruel rulers, Avraham discovered the idea of one God—a God of kindness to all human beings, a God of peace among all people. Avraham was a great "discoverer." The idea that he discovered is the basis of three great religions. The idea of one God shook the world and influences all of our lives to this day.

The world has made much progress because of great discoveries of all kinds—discoveries made by rabbis, scientists, doctors, inventors, philosophers, and artists. These discoveries have made our lives healthier, safer, happier, and more meaningful.

Think of three great discoverers whose ideas, inventions, or discoveries have influenced the way we live today.

NAME_____
IDEA or INVENTION or DISCOVERY_____
BENEFIT TO HUMANITY

NAME_____
IDEA or INVENTION or DISCOVERY_____
BENEFIT TO HUMANITY

NAME_____
IDEA or INVENTION or DISCOVERY_____
BENEFIT TO HUMANITY

One God

The belief in one God is the first and most basic idea of Judaism. It is a belief that Avraham came to on his own after long, hard thought. He saw that there was one God who was the creator of the world and of the human race. Because humans have a spirit and can think and feel and tell right from wrong, Avraham understood that humans were made in the image of God. Avraham taught others his ideas. They, too, saw that he must be right. This was the beginning of Judaism.

You may find it hard to understand how people could ever have believed in many gods. But many, many years ago most people did not believe in one God. They saw the beautiful, fiery sun and thought it surely must be a god. They felt a chilling, powerful wind. "Is not this a god?" they asked. It took the keen mind of Avram to realize that one great power must be guiding all the powerful forces of nature. He understood that there must be one God.

Today all the great religions of the world tell of the one God. Each religion has its own understanding of the nature of God, and Judaism is our way. We have believed in one God since the time of Avraham. And today, when you think about the idea of one God, you can almost feel the joy and wonder that Avraham knew when he first saw the truth.

What Do You Think?

1. Do you ever think about how nature works? Does it seem miraculous to you?
2. How do you think Avraham came to realize that there must be one God?
3. Do you believe in one God?
4. Which religion was the first with the belief in one God?
5. Could Judaism exist without the belief in one God?
6. For whom do we perform all our מִצְווֹת?

וְאָהַבְתָּ אֵת יְיָ אֱלֹהֶיךָ
And You Shall Love the Eternal, Your God

Knowing the Prayer Vocabulary

לְבָבְךָ	your heart	וְאָהַבְתָּ	and you shall love
לֵבָב	heart	אָהַב	he loved
נַפְשְׁךָ	your soul	אֱלֹהֶיךָ	your God
נֶפֶשׁ	soul	אֱלֹהִים	God
מְאֹדֶךָ	your might	וּבְכָל	and with all
מְאֹד	might, much	כָּל	all

Knowing the Words
Circle the correct Hebrew word.

1. with all	בָּרוּךְ	לֶחֶם	בְּכָל
2. your God	אֱלֹהֶיךָ	אֱלֹהֵינוּ	הַמּוֹצִיא
3. he loved	אֱלֹהֵינוּ	מֶלֶךְ	אָהַב
4. God	אֱלֹהִים	אַתָּה	הָעוֹלָם
5. your heart	מִן	לְבָבְךָ	אֶחָד
6. your soul	הָאָרֶץ	נַפְשְׁךָ	שְׁמַע
7. heart	לֵבָב	וָעֶד	מַלְכוּתוֹ
8. soul	לִקְרַאת	יִשְׂרָאֵל	נֶפֶשׁ
9. and you shall love	לְעוֹלָם	בָּרוּךְ	וְאָהַבְתָּ
10. your might	שֵׁם	מְאֹדֶךָ	כָּבוֹד

In the paragraph that follows the *Shema* we express our love for God, promising to remember God's teachings at all times and to follow God's law.

And you shall love the Eternal, your God   וְאָהַבְתָּ אֵת יְיָ אֱלֹהֶיךָ

    with all your heart,   בְּכָל־לְבָבְךָ
    and with all your soul,   וּבְכָל־נַפְשְׁךָ
    and with all your might.   וּבְכָל־מְאֹדֶךָ.

Knowing the Phrases
Draw a line from the Hebrew phrase to its English meaning.

1. and with all your soul   וְאָהַבְתָּ אֵת יְיָ אֱלֹהֶיךָ
2. and with all your might   בְּכָל־לְבָבְךָ
3. And you shall love the Eternal your God   וּבְכָל־מְאֹדֶךָ
4. with all your heart   וּבְכָל־נַפְשְׁךָ

This sentence in the שְׁמַע יִשְׂרָאֵל prayer commands us to love God with all of our hearts, all our souls and all our might.
The rabbis say that the word מְאֹדֶךָ, refers to "your possessions." In other words, we are commanded to use our possessions. We can do this by helping people and institutions which are in need of God's service.

$$\text{וְאָהַבְתָּ אֵת יְיָ אֱלֹהֶיךָ, בְּכָל לְבָבְךָ,}$$
$$\text{וּבְכָל נַפְשְׁךָ, וּבְכָל מְאֹדֶךָ.}$$

See page 157 for the complete/שְׁמַע

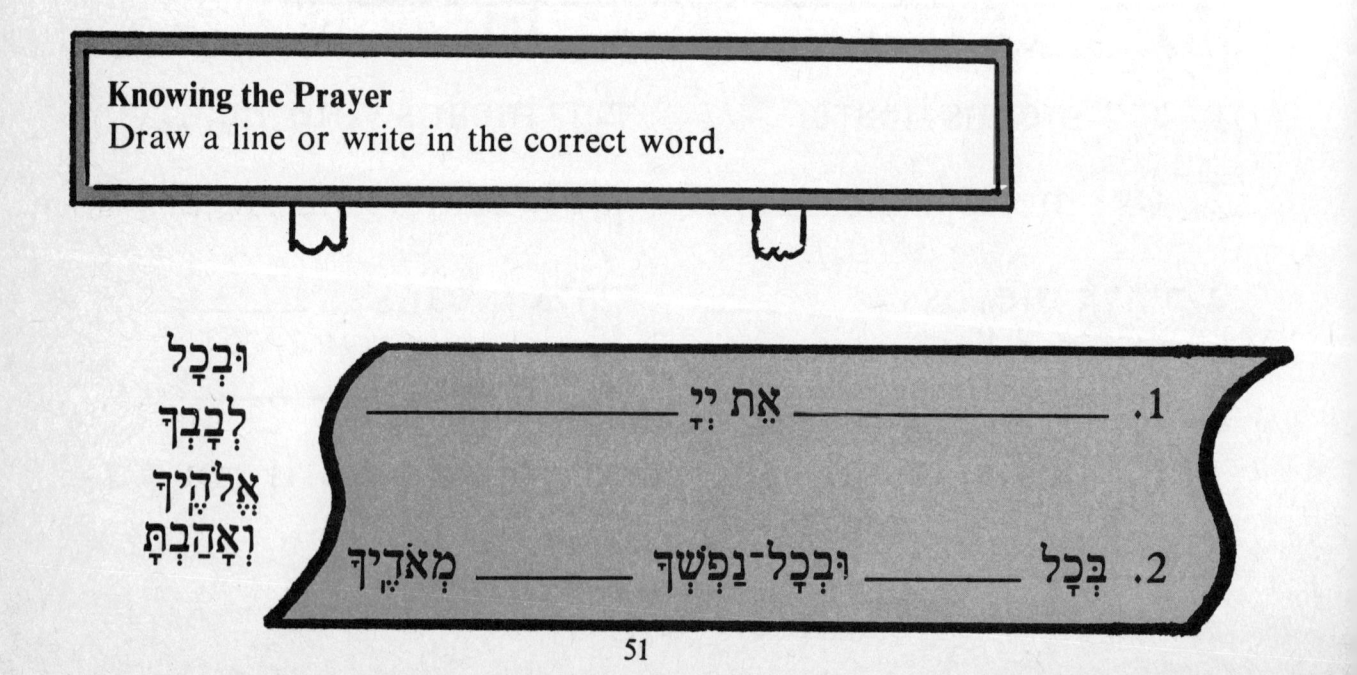

Knowing the Prayer
Draw a line or write in the correct word.

וּבְכָל
לְבָבְךָ
אֱלֹהֶיךָ
וְאָהַבְתָּ

1. _____ אֵת יְיָ _____

2. בְּכָל _____ וּבְכָל־נַפְשְׁךָ _____ מְאֹדֶךָ

Knowing the Answers
Write your answer to each of the questions.

1. How can you love God with all your heart and with all your soul?
_____
_____

2. How can you love God with all your possessions?
_____
_____

3. What does the *Shema* teach us about *tzedakah*?
_____

Knowing the Suffixes
Fill in the missing words.

1. לֵבָב means heart　　לְבָבְךָ means your heart

2. נֶפֶשׁ means _____　　נַפְשְׁךָ means _____

3. אֱלֹהִים means _____　　אֱלֹהֶיךָ means _____

4. בַּיִת means _____　　בֵּיתֶךָ means _____

The suffix ךָ at the end of a word means _____.

Acts of Love

The first sentence of the שְׁמַע tells us to love the Eternal with all our heart and with all our soul.

We show our love for God by praying and showing respect for all God's creations.

Make a list of loving things that you can do in the next several weeks—acts of love that you can do for your family, for your friends, for yourself, for neighbors, and for someone you don't even know.

1. Someone tells a lie about you.

_____

_____

2. Someone scratches your favorite record.

_____

_____

3. A friend blabs one of your secrets.

_____

_____

4. You are blamed by someone for something you did not do.
_____
_____

5. Someone puts salt in your soft drink.
_____
_____

6. Someone hides your books.
_____
_____

7. Someone refuses to give you the homework assignment for the next school day.
_____
_____

8. Someone refuses to help you with your homework.
_____
_____

9. Add your own examples.
_____
_____

10. Did the person who harmed you ask you to forgive him or her?
_____
_____

How did that person ask your forgiveness?
_____
_____

מִי־כָמֹכָה?
Who Is Like You?

Knowing the Prayer Vocabulary

בַּקֹדֶשׁ	in holiness	מִי־כָמֹכָה	who is like you
נוֹרָא	awesome	כְּמוֹ	like, as
תְהִלוֹת	splendid	בָּאֵלִים	among mighty (gods)
עֹשֵׂה	doing	אֵל	God
עָשָׂה	he did	נֶאְדָּר	great
פֶּלֶא	miracle(s), wonder(s)		

Knowing the Words
Circle the correct Hebrew word.

1. among the gods	בָּאֵלִים	כָּמְכָה	מִי	
2. like, as	תְהִלֹּת	עֹשֵׂה	כְּמוֹ	
3. like you	נֶאְדָּר	כָמְכָה	נוֹרָא	
4. miracle(s), wonder(s)	לִקְרַאת	בָּאֵלִים	פֶּלֶא	
5. great	נֶאְדָּר	בַּקֹּדֶשׁ	בְּךָ	
6. in holiness	מִי־כָמְכָה	וּבְכָל־	בַּקֹּדֶשׁ	
7. awesome	אֶת	וּבְכָל	נוֹרָא	
8. splendid	תְהִלֹּת	כַּלָּה	פְּנֵי	
9. doing	לְכָה	עֹשֵׂה	שַׁבָּת	
10. he did	לִקְרַאת	עָשָׂה	דּוֹדִי	

The prayer מִי־כָמֹכָה is from the Bible. It is the hymn of praise that Moses sang to God after he led the Israelites across the Red Sea.

Who is like You	מִי־כָמֹכָה
among the mighty (gods)?	בָּאֵלִים יְיָ?
Who is like You	מִי כָּמֹכָה
great in holiness?	נֶאְדָּר בַּקֹּדֶשׁ?
Impressive and splendid	נוֹרָא תְהִלֹּת
doing wonders.	עֹשֵׂה פֶלֶא.

Knowing the Phrases
Draw a line from the Hebrew phrase to its English meaning.

1. doing wonders   נֶאְדָּר בַּקֹּדֶשׁ

2. who is like You   עֹשֵׂא פֶלֶא

3. great in holiness   מִי־כָמֹכָה

The whole world is filled with God's wonders.

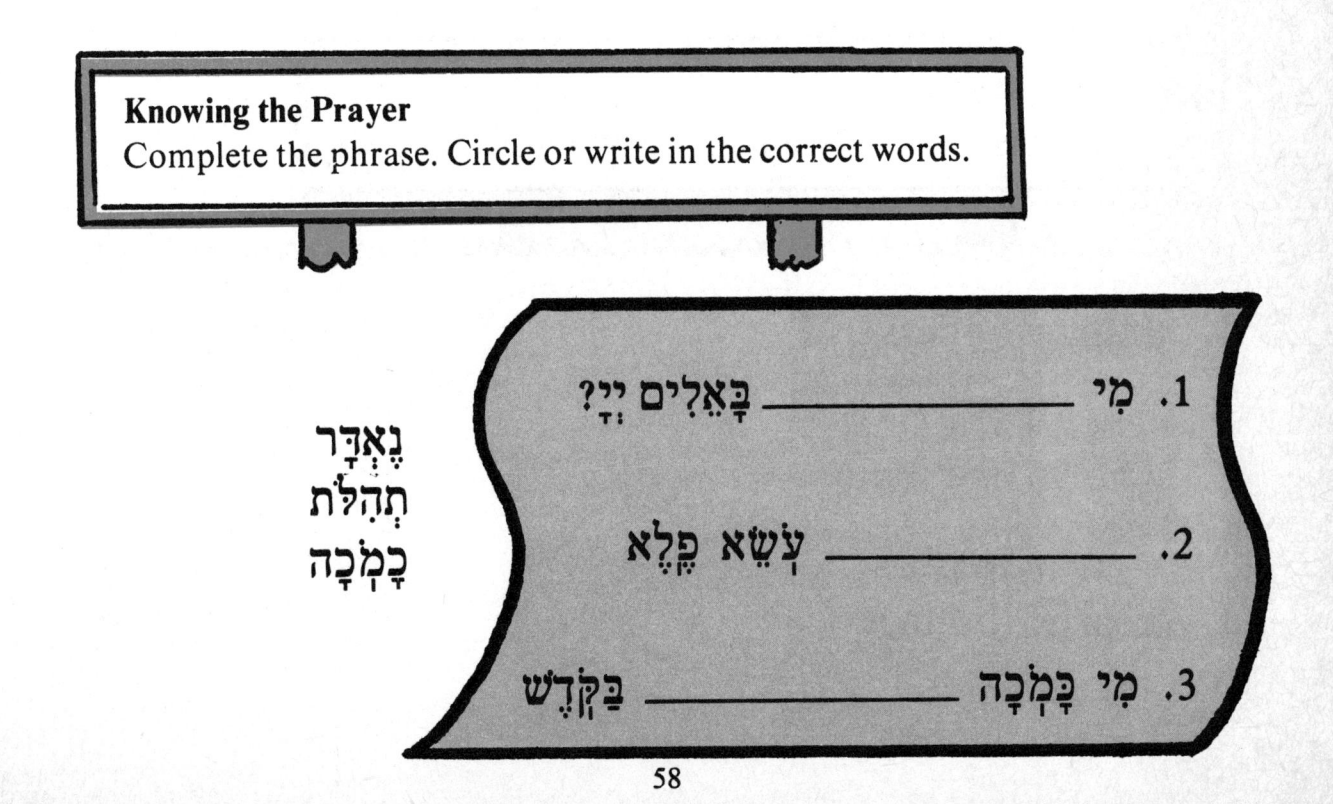

מִי־כָמֹכָה בָּאֵלִם יְיָ?
מִי כָּמֹכָה נֶאְדָּר בַּקֹּדֶשׁ?
נוֹרָא תְהִלֹּת, עֹשֵׂה פֶלֶא!

Knowing the Prayer
Complete the phrase. Circle or write in the correct words.

1. מִי _____ בָּאֵלִים יְיָ?

2. _____ עֹשֵׂא פֶלֶא

3. מִי כָמֹכָה _____ בַּקֹּדֶשׁ

נֶאְדָּר
תְהִלֹּת
כָמֹכָה

Knowing the Hebrew Phrases
Fill in the missing translations.

1. שָׁלוֹם means peace   עוֹשֶׂה שָׁלוֹם means who makes peace

2. חֹשֶׁךְ means _____   עוֹשֶׂה חֹשֶׁךְ means _____

3. אוֹר means _____   עוֹשֶׂה אוֹר means _____

The word עוֹשֶׂה means _____

Knowing the Answers
Write your answer to each of the questions.

1. Is there anyone as great as God?
_____
_____

2. Are you capable of performing wonders?
_____
_____

3. Who is capable of performing wonders?
_____
_____

יְצִיאַת מִצְרַיִם
The Exodus

Story Vocabulary

בְּנֵי יִשְׂרָאֵל	Children of Israel	מִצְרִים	Egyptian
יַם סוּף	Red Sea	מִצְרַיִם	Egypt
עַמוּד הָאֵשׁ	pillar of fire	מֹשֶׁה	Moses
פַּרְעֹה	Pharaoh	עָנָן	cloud
		פָּרָשִׁים	horsemen

Suddenly, early in the morning, the בְּנֵי יִשְׂרָאֵל went out of the land after 210 years in מִצְרַיִם. They went out in order, like a great army, family by family and tribe by tribe.

And God went before the people of יִשְׂרָאֵל to guide them as they marched out of the land of מִצְרַיִם. In the daytime they were guided by a עָנָן, like a pillar, in front, and at night by an עַמוּד הָאֵשׁ. So both by day and night, as they saw the cloud and the עַמוּד הָאֵשׁ going before them, they could say, "Our Lord, the God of heaven and earth, goes before us."

When the pillar of עָנָן stopped, they knew it was a sign that they were to pause in their journey and rest. So they set up their tents and waited until the עָנָן should rise up and go forward. When they looked and saw that the pillar of עָנָן was higher up in the air, and as though moving forward, they took down their tents and formed in order for the march. Thus the עָנָן was like a guide by day and a guard by night.

After the בְּנֵי יִשְׂרָאֵל had left מִצְרַיִם, פַּרְעֹה missed his slaves, saying:

"What have we done, to let our slaves go?"

60

He was afraid, too, that such a large number of people might join up with his enemies. So פַּרְעֹה ordered his army to prepare, and chased the בְּנֵי יִשְׂרָאֵל. The בְּנֵי יִשְׂרָאֵל were encamped to prepare to rest beside the יַם סוּף, when they saw a great cloud of dust on the horizon. Then someone shouted:

"We are lost! It is the army of פַּרְעֹה come to take us back to slavery!"

"Fear not," declared מֹשֶׁה. "Stand still and see how God will save you. The Lord will fight for you, and you shall stand still and see your enemies slain."

That night the עַמּוּד הָאֵשׁ which was before the people of יִשְׂרָאֵל went behind them and stood between the camp of the מִצְרִים and the camp of the בְּנֵי יִשְׂרָאֵל. To the יִשְׂרָאֵל it was bright and dazzling with the glory of God, but to the מִצְרִים the pillar was dark and terrible, and they dared not enter it.

And all that night there blew over the sea a mighty east wind, so that the water was blown away; and when the morning came, there was a ridge of dry land between water on one side and the water on the other, making a road across the sea to the land beyond, and on each side of the road the water stood like walls, as if to keep their enemies away from them.

Then מֹשֶׁה told the people to go forward. They walked across the יַם סוּף as on dry land and passed safely over into the wilderness on the other side. So God brought his people out of מִצְרַיִם into a land that they had never seen.

When the מִצְרִים saw them marching into the sea, they followed with their פָּרָשִׁים. But the sand was no longer hard; it had become soft, and the chariot wheels were caught in it, and many wheels broke off. And the פָּרָשִׁים sank in the mud and fell down, so that the army was in confusion; and all were frightened. The soldiers cried out:

"Let us run away from the בְּנֵי יִשְׂרָאֵל! The Lord is fighting for them and against us!"

By this time, all the בְּנֵי יִשְׂרָאֵל had passed through the יַם סוּף and were standing on the high ground beyond it, looking at their enemies slowly struggling through the sand, all in one heaped-up mass of men and chariots and פָּרָשִׁים. Then מֹשֶׁה lifted up his hand, and at once a great tide of water swept up from the sea. The hard road over which the בְּנֵי יִשְׂרָאֵל had walked in safety was now covered with water; and the army of פַּרְעֹה, with all his פָּרָשִׁים were drowned in the יַם סוּף, before the eyes of the בְּנֵי יִשְׂרָאֵל.

The exodus from מִצְרַיִם was one of the most important events in Jewish history. This prayer ties us to our past and helps us to remember that God has watched over the Jewish people in all lands and all ages.

The בְּנֵי יִשְׂרָאֵל praised God and sang a song of victory:

אָשִׁירָה לַיהֹוָה	I will sing to the Eternal,
כִּי־גָאֹה גָּאָה.	For He has triumphed.
סוּס וְרֹכְבוֹ רָמָה	He has drowned horse and rider
בַיָּם.	In the sea.
מִי־כָמֹכָה	Who is like You
בָּאֵלִים יְהֹוָה?	Among the mighty, O Lord?
מִי כָּמֹכָה	Who is like You,
נֶאְדָּר בַּקֹּדֶשׁ?	Great in holiness?

God saved the בְּנֵי יִשְׂרָאֵל from the pursuing Egyptian army by drowning them in the rushing waters of the יַם סוּף

The Midrash tells us that when the angels in Heaven witnessed the crossing of the יַם סוּף, they began to sing songs of praise to the Almighty.

But God silenced them immediately.

The Eternal said, "The מִצְרִים are also my creations. Do not sing and rejoice while my creatures are dying."

וְשָׁמְרוּ בְנֵי־יִשְׂרָאֵל אֶת־הַשַׁבָּת
The Children of Israel Shall Keep Shabbat

Knowing the Prayer Vocabulary

בֵּין	between	שָׁמְרוּ	And they shall keep
אוֹת	sign	שָׁמַר	he preserved, he kept
שֵׁשֶׁת	six	לַעֲשׂוֹת	to observe, to do
יָמִים	days	עָשָׂה	he observed, he did
יוֹם	day	לְדֹרֹתָם	for their generations
הַשָּׁמַיִם	the heavens	דֹר, דוֹר	generation
יוֹם הַשְּׁבִיעִי	the seventh day	בְּרִית עוֹלָם	everlasting covenant
שָׁבַת	he rested	בְּרִית	covenant
וַיִּנָּפַשׁ	he stopped	בֵּינִי	between me

Knowing the Words
Circle the correct Hebrew word.

1. the heavens   אוֹת   הַשָּׁמַיִם   בְּרִית

2. sign   וּבֵין   בֵּינִי   אוֹת

3.	he preserved, he kept	הִיא	בְּרִית	שָׁמַר
4.	covenant	בְּרִית	וּבַיּוֹם	בֵּינִי
5.	generation	דֹּר	יָמִים	אוֹת
6.	he did	עוֹלָם	עָשָׂה	בֵּין
7.	to observe, to do	שָׁבַת	הַזְּמַנִּים	לַעֲשׂוֹת
8.	and they shall keep	שָׁמְרוּ	שֵׁשֶׁת	יוֹם
9.	between	דֹּר	בֵּין	הַשְּׁבִיעִי
10.	for their generations	הַשַּׁבָּת	אֶת	לְדֹרֹתָם
11.	between me	אֶת	בֵּינִי	וְשָׁמְרוּ
12.	day	הַשַּׁבָּת	יוֹם	עוֹלָם
13.	six	שָׁמְרוּ	הִיא	שֵׁשֶׁת
14.	the seventh day	יוֹם הַשְּׁבִיעִי	לַעֲשׂוֹת	הַשְּׁבִיעִי
15.	he stopped	שָׁבַת	לְעוֹלָם	אֶת־הַשַּׁבָּת
16.	days	לְדֹרֹתָם	יָמִים	וַיִּנָּפַשׁ
17.	he rested	שָׁבַת	נָפַשׁ	וַיִּנָּפַשׁ
18.	everlasting covenant	בְּרִית עוֹלָם	בְּנֵי־יִשְׂרָאֵל	בְּנֵי־יִשְׂרָאֵל

There is no special Hebrew name in the Jewish calendar for any day of the week except Shabbat, the day of rest.

The people of Israel shall keep the Shabbat	וְשָׁמְרוּ בְנֵי־יִשְׂרָאֵל אֶת־הַשַּׁבָּת,
to observe the Shabbat for their generations	לַעֲשׂוֹת אֶת הַשַּׁבָּת לְדֹרֹתָם,
as an everlasting covenant.	בְּרִית עוֹלָם.
Between Me and the children of Israel	בֵּינִי וּבֵין בְּנֵי־יִשְׂרָאֵל
it is a sign forever,	אוֹת הִיא לְעוֹלָם,
for in six days God created	כִּי־שֵׁשֶׁת יָמִים עָשָׂה יְיָ
the heavens and the earth	אֶת־הַשָּׁמַיִם וְאֶת־הָאָרֶץ,
and on the seventh day	וּבַיּוֹם הַשְּׁבִיעִי
God rested and stopped.	שָׁבַת וַיִּנָּפַשׁ.

Knowing the Phrases
Draw a line from the Hebrew phrase to its English meaning.

1. and on the seventh day — עָשָׂה יְיָ אֶת־הַשָּׁמַיִם

2. God created the heavens — לַעֲשׂוֹת אֶת הַשַּׁבָּת לְדֹרֹתָם,

3. to observe the Shabbat — בְּנֵי־יִשְׂרָאֵל

4. the children of Israel — וּבַיּוֹם הַשְּׁבִיעִי

The תּוֹרָה tells us that God created the world in six days. On the seventh day, God rested from the work of creation. In commemoration, with too rest on the seventh day of the week—שַׁבָּת.

וְשָׁמְרוּ בְנֵי־יִשְׂרָאֵל אֶת־הַשַּׁבָּת.
לַעֲשׂוֹת אֶת הַשַּׁבָּת לְדֹרֹתָם, בְּרִית עוֹלָם:
בֵּינִי וּבֵין בְּנֵי־יִשְׂרָאֵל אוֹת הִיא לְעוֹלָם,
כִּי־שֵׁשֶׁת יָמִים עָשָׂה יְיָ אֶת־הַשָּׁמַיִם
וְאֶת־הָאָרֶץ, וּבַיּוֹם הַשְּׁבִיעִי שָׁבַת וַיִּנָּפַשׁ.

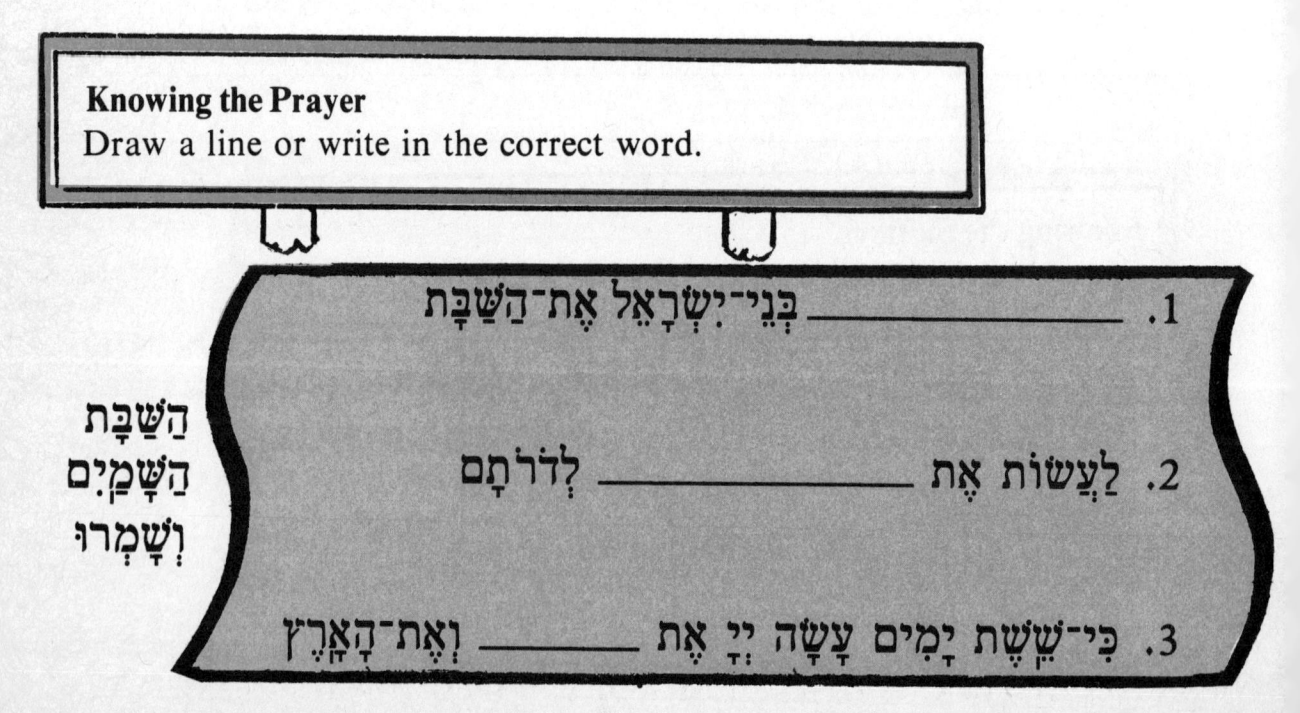

Knowing the Prayer
Draw a line or write in the correct word.

1. _____ בְּנֵי־יִשְׂרָאֵל אֶת־הַשַּׁבָּת

הַשַּׁבָּת
הַשָּׁמַיִם
וְשָׁמְרוּ

2. לַעֲשׂוֹת אֶת _____ לְדֹרֹתָם

3. כִּי־שֵׁשֶׁת יָמִים עָשָׂה יְיָ אֶת _____ וְאֶת־הָאָרֶץ

67

Knowing the Answers
Write your answer to each of the questions.

1. In how many days did God create the world?
   _____
   _____

2. What did God do on the seventh day?
   _____
   _____

3. Which nation was chosen to preserve the Sabbath?
   _____
   _____

4. What is the everlasting covenant between God and Israel?
   _____
   _____

Knowing the Suffixes
Fill in the missing words.

1. יוֹם means day   יָמִים means days
2. מֶלֶךְ means _____   מְלָכִים means _____
3. גֶּפֶן means _____   גְּפָנִים means _____

The suffix ים‎x at the end of a word means _____

The Torah and You

A בְּרִית is a covenant or a promise to care for or to help someone or something. A teacher has a בְּרִית with his or her pupils. A parent has a covenant with his or her family.

How do each of these people honor their covenant? Doctors, teachers, students, rabbis, playmates, sisters, brothers, bosses, storekeepers, employees, children, police officers, sanitation workers, teammates.

RABBI	DOCTOR

SANITATION MAN	TEACHER

עָלֵינוּ לְשַׁבֵּחַ
It is Our Duty

Knowing the Prayer Vocabulary

עָלֵינוּ	it is our duty [on us]	כְּגוֹיֵי	like the nations of
עַל	on	גוֹי	nation
לְשַׁבֵּחַ	to praise	הָאֲרָצוֹת	the lands
לַאֲדוֹן	to the Master	אֶרֶץ	land
אָדוֹן	Master	שָׂמָנוּ	placed us
גְּדֻלָּה	greatness	שָׂם	he placed
לְיוֹצֵר בְּרֵאשִׁית	to the Creator	כְּמִשְׁפְּחוֹת	like the families
שֶׁלֹּא	who has not	מִשְׁפָּחָה	family
עָשָׂנוּ	made us	הָאֲדָמָה	earth
עָשָׂה	he made		

Knowing the Words
Circle the correct Hebrew words.

1. placed us   קִדְּשָׁנוּ   אֱלֹהֵינוּ   שָׂמָנוּ

2. he placed	שָׁם	בָּאֵלִים	פֶּלֶא
3. like the families	עָשָׂה	כְּמִשְׁפְּחוֹת	תְּהִלֹּת
4. family	מִשְׁפָּחָה	שָׂרָה	אַבְרָהָם
5. it is our duty [on us]	אַתָּה	נוֹרָא	עָלֵינוּ
6. on	עַל	נֶאְדָּר	כָּמֹכָה
7. to praise	לְהַדְלִיק	לְשַׁבֵּחַ	נֵר
8. the lands	הָאֲרָצוֹת	לְכָה	שַׁבֵּחַ
9. to the Master	לַאֲדוֹן	נְקַבְּלָה	שַׁבָּת
10. Master of	דּוֹדִי	פְּנֵי	אָדוֹן
11. greatness	גְּדֻלָּה	בָּרְכוּ	הַמְבֹרָךְ
12. to the Creator	לְיוֹצֵר בְּרֵאשִׁית	שֶׁל־שַׁבָּת	אֶת־יְיָ
13. who has not	וָעֶד	שֶׁלֹּא	לְעוֹלָם
14. made us	עָשָׂנוּ	מַה־טֹּבוּ	יַעֲקֹב
15. he made	כַּלָּה	אֹהָלֶיךָ	עָשָׂה
16. like the nations	כְּגוֹיֵי	מִי־כָמֹכָה	לַאֲדוֹן
17. nation	לִקְרַאת	גּוֹי	אֲשֶׁר

For over 600 years the עָלֵינוּ has been the closing prayer in the services of all congregations on weekdays, Sabbaths, and holidays.

In the עָלֵינוּ we recognize God as the Creator of the world.

We bow our heads as we worship and praise God. We pray that one day the entire human race will recognize that there is one God who rules the world.

It is our duty to praise the Master of all,	עָלֵינוּ לְשַׁבֵּחַ לַאֲדוֹן הַכֹּל,
to give greatness	לָתֵת גְּדֻלָּה
to the Creator	לְיוֹצֵר בְּרֵאשִׁית,
The Eternal has not made us	שֶׁלֹּא עָשָׂנוּ
like the nations of other lands.	כְּגוֹיֵי הָאֲרָצוֹת,
And has not placed us	וְלֹא שָׂמָנוּ
like the families of earth.	כְּמִשְׁפְּחוֹת הָאֲדָמָה.

Knowing the Phrases
Draw a line from the Hebrew phrase to its English meaning.

1. like nations of other lands   לָתֵת גְּדֻלָּה
2. like the families of earth   כְּמִשְׁפְּחוֹת הָאֲדָמָה
3. it is our duty to praise   כְּגוֹיֵי הָאֲרָצוֹת
4. He has not made us   וְלֹא שָׂמָנוּ
5. to give greatness   עָלֵינוּ לְשַׁבֵּחַ

The עָלֵינוּ prayer closes all congregation's services on weekdays, Sabbaths and Festivals.

עָלֵינוּ לְשַׁבֵּחַ לַאֲדוֹן הַכֹּל, לָתֵת גְּדֻלָּה לְיוֹצֵר בְּרֵאשִׁית, שֶׁלֹּא עָשָׂנוּ כְּגוֹיֵי הָאֲרָצוֹת, וְלֹא שָׂמָנוּ כְּמִשְׁפְּחוֹת הָאֲדָמָה.

See page 159 for the עָלֵינוּ

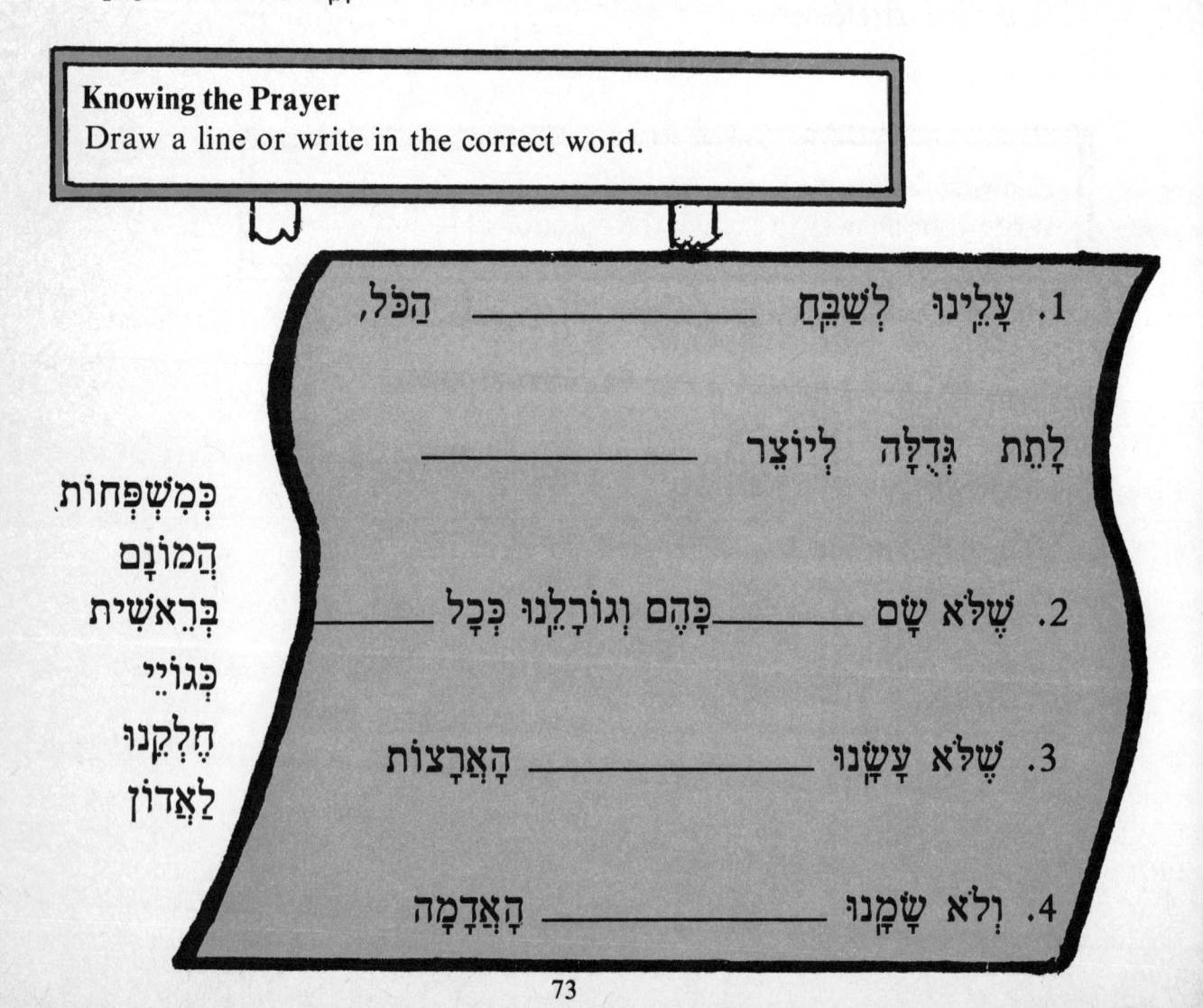

Knowing the Prayer
Draw a line or write in the correct word.

1. עָלֵינוּ לְשַׁבֵּחַ _____ הַכֹּל,

   לָתֵת גְּדֻלָּה לְיוֹצֵר _____

כְּמִשְׁפְּחוֹת
הֲמוֹנָם
בְּרֵאשִׁית
כְּגוֹיֵי
חֶלְקֵנוּ
לַאֲדוֹן

2. שֶׁלֹּא שָׂם _____ כָּהֶם וְגוֹרָלֵנוּ כְּכָל

3. שֶׁלֹּא עָשָׂנוּ _____ הָאֲרָצוֹת

4. וְלֹא שָׂמָנוּ _____ הָאֲדָמָה

73

Knowing the Ideas
Draw a line from the Hebrew phrase to its English meaning.

1. it is our duty to praise God   עָלֵינוּ לְשַׁבֵּחַ לַאֲדוֹן הַכֹּל

2. we recognize God's greatness   וְלֹא שָׂמָנוּ כְּמִשְׁפְּחוֹת הָאֲדָמָה

3. we are different   לָתֵת גְּדֻלָּה לְיוֹצֵר בְּרֵאשִׁית

Knowing the Answers
Write your answer to each of the questions.

1. How do we praise God?
   _____
   _____

2. What makes the Jewish religion different than other religions?
   _____
   _____

Knowing the Suffixes
Fill in the missing translations.

1. גוֹרָל means lot   גוֹרָלֵנוּ means our lot
2. חֵלֶק means _____   חֶלְקֵנוּ means _____
3. אָדוֹן means _____   אֲדוֹנֵנוּ means _____

The suffix נוּ at the end of a word means _____

Knowing the Suffixes
Fill in the missing translations.

1. מִשְׁפָּחָה means family   מִשְׁפָּחוֹת means families
2. אֶרֶץ means _____   אֲרָצוֹת means _____
3. מִצְוָה means _____   מִצְווֹת means _____
4. תּוֹרָה means _____   תּוֹרוֹת means _____

The suffix וֹת at the end of a word means [feminine] _____.

We See God's Work in the World

No one can ever see God, because God has no body or shape or form. But we do see God's work in the world, and we know that God is there.

We see order in the world of nature and know this is God's plan. Day follows night and night follows day. And it will be so forever. This is an order we can depend on; we know it will always be so. The seasons, spring and summer and autumn and winter, follow each other in that order and always will.

We see God's work in the variety that's in the world. There are many kinds of flowers and animals and people in the world. List three ways in which they are alike and three ways in which they are different from each other:

Animals—Alike

1. _____
2. _____
3. _____

Animals—Different

1. _____
2. _____
3. _____

People—Alike

1. _____
2. _____
3. _____

People—Different

1. _____
2. _____
3. _____

The Names of God

There are many Hebrew names for God. Each of these names tells us something about what we think of God.

What Do You Think?

God is also called אֲדוֹן הַכֹּל.
What does this name tell us about what we think of God?

Another name is יוֹצֵר בְּרֵאשִׁית.
What does this name tell us about what we think of God?

Another name for God is מֶלֶךְ הָעוֹלָם.
What does this name tell us about how we think of God?

Another name for God is אֱלֹהֵינוּ.
What two words do you see in this name?
What does this name tell us about how we think of God?

אֵין כֵּאלֹהֵינוּ
There is None Like Our God

Knowing the Prayer Vocabulary

מֶלֶךְ	ruler	אֵין	there is none
כְּמוֹשִׁיעֵנוּ	our helper	כֵּאלֹהֵינוּ	like our God
מוֹשִׁיעַ	helper	אֱלֹהִים	God
מִי	who is	כְּ, כָּ	like
נוֹדֶה	let us give thanks	כַּאדוֹנֵינוּ	like our holy one
הוֹדָה	to thank	אָדוֹן	holy one
בָּרוּךְ	blessed	כְּמַלְכֵּנוּ	like our ruler
אַתָּה	you (are)		

Knowing the Words
Circle the correct Hebrew word.

1. ruler — אֵין · נוֹדֶה · מֶלֶךְ
2. our helper — מוֹשִׁיעֵנוּ · מַלְכֵּנוּ · נְקַבְּלָה
3. helper — נוֹדֶה · מוֹשִׁיעַ · כֵּאלֹהֵינוּ
4. let us give thanks — הַמְבֹרָךְ · אֶת־יְיָ · נוֹדֶה
5. thanks — תּוֹדָה · וָעֶד · לֵאלֹהֵינוּ
6. there is none — אֵין · לְעוֹלָם · מַלְכֵּנוּ
7. like our holy one — בָּרוּךְ · בָּרְכוּ · אֲדוֹנֵינוּ
8. holy one — אָדוֹן · נוֹדֶה · אַתָּה
9. like our ruler — כְּמַלְכֵּנוּ · בָּרוּךְ · לַאדוֹנֵינוּ

The אֵין כֵּאלֹהֵינוּ is very old. We chant it every Sabbath and holiday. It uses four different names for God: אֱלֹהֵנוּ, אֲדוֹנֵינוּ, מַלְכֵּנוּ, and מוֹשִׁיעֵנוּ. The first letters of the three verses make up the word אָמֵן.

1. אֵין כֵּאלֹהֵינוּ,   There is none like our God.
    אֵין כַּאדוֹנֵינוּ,   There is none like our holy one.
    אֵין כְּמַלְכֵּנוּ,   There is none like our ruler.
    אֵין כְּמוֹשִׁיעֵנוּ.   There is none like our helper.

2. מִי כֵאלֹהֵינוּ,   Who is like our God?
    מִי כַאדוֹנֵינוּ,   Who is like our holy one.
    מִי כְמַלְכֵּנוּ,   Who is like our ruler?
    מִי כְמוֹשִׁיעֵנוּ.   Who is like our helper?

3. נוֹדֶה לֵאלֹהֵינוּ,   Let us give thanks to our God.
    נוֹדֶה לַאדוֹנֵינוּ,   Let us give thanks to our holy one.
    נוֹדֶה לְמַלְכֵּנוּ,   Let us give thanks to our ruler.
    נוֹדֶה לְמוֹשִׁיעֵנוּ.   Let us give thanks to our helper.

4. בָּרוּךְ אֱלֹהֵינוּ,   Praised be our God.
    בָּרוּךְ אֲדוֹנֵינוּ,   Praised be our holy one.
    בָּרוּךְ מַלְכֵּנוּ,   Praised be our ruler.
    בָּרוּךְ מוֹשִׁיעֵנוּ.   Praised be our helper.

5. אַתָּה הוּא אֱלֹהֵינוּ,   You are our God.
   אַתָּה הוּא אֲדוֹנֵינוּ,   You are our holy one.
   אַתָּה הוּא מַלְכֵּנוּ,   You are our ruler.
   אַתָּה הוּא מוֹשִׁיעֵנוּ.   You are our helper.

The words of אֵין כֵּאלֹהֵינוּ repeat themselves. By knowing just a few words, you can understand the entire hymn. Match word and meaning:

_____   אֱלֹהֵינוּ   A. our God

_____   אֲדוֹנֵינוּ   B. our helper

_____   מַלְכֵּנוּ   C. our ruler

_____   מוֹשִׁיעֵנוּ   D. like

_____   כְּ ...   E. to

_____   לְ ...   F. our holy one

_____   אֵין   A. who (is)?

_____   מִי   B. we will give thanks

_____   נוֹדֶה   C. you (are)

_____   בָּרוּךְ   D. (there is) none

_____   אַתָּה   E. blessed (is)

In the last verse, we show how close we feel toward God, when we say, "You are our God, our holy one, our ruler, and our helper."

1. אֵין כֵּאלֹהֵינוּ, אֵין כַּאדוֹנֵינוּ,
אֵין כְּמַלְכֵּנוּ, אֵין כְּמוֹשִׁיעֵנוּ.

2. מִי כֵאלֹהֵינוּ, מִי כַאדוֹנֵינוּ,
מִי כְמַלְכֵּנוּ, מִי כְמוֹשִׁיעֵנוּ.

3. נוֹדֶה לֵאלֹהֵינוּ, נוֹדֶה לַאדוֹנֵינוּ,
נוֹדֶה לְמַלְכֵּנוּ, נוֹדֶה לְמוֹשִׁיעֵנוּ.

4. בָּרוּךְ אֱלֹהֵינוּ, בָּרוּךְ אֲדוֹנֵינוּ,
בָּרוּךְ מַלְכֵּנוּ, בָּרוּךְ מוֹשִׁיעֵנוּ.

5. אַתָּה הוּא אֱלֹהֵינוּ, אַתָּה הוּא אֲדוֹנֵינוּ,
אַתָּה הוּא מַלְכֵּנוּ, אַתָּה הוּא מוֹשִׁיעֵנוּ.

Each stanza consisting of four phrases, begins with a different letter repeated four times. Mark those letters here.

Stanza 1 _____

Stanza 2 _____

Stanza 3 _____

Stanza 4 _____

Stanza 5 _____

The letters from stanzas 1, 2, and 3 spell out a familiar word of prayer. What is that word?

_____

The letters from stanzas 4 and 5 may possibly be an abbreviation for the first two of the six words with which בְּרָכוֹת begin. Show how this is so.

_____

This type of poetic writing is called "acrostic." Sometimes it is alphabetical. Sometimes it is used to spell out an author's name.

Knowing the Prefixes
Fill in the missing translations.

1. אֱלֹהֵינוּ means our God   כֵּאלֹהֵינוּ means like our God
2. אֲדוֹנֵינוּ means our ____   כַּאדוֹנֵינוּ means ____
3. מַלְכֵּנוּ means our ____   כְּמַלְכֵּנוּ means ____
4. מוֹשִׁיעֵנוּ means our ____   כְּמוֹשִׁיעֵנוּ means ____

The prefix כְּ or כַּ or כֵּ before a word means _____.

Knowing the Phrases
Draw a line from the Hebrew phrase to its English meaning.

1. Who is like our helper?   אֵין כְּמַלְכֵּנוּ
2. Praised be our God   אַתָּה הוּא אֲדוֹנֵינוּ
3. You are our holy one   נוֹדֶה לַאדוֹנֵינוּ
4. Let us give thanks to our holy one   בָּרוּךְ אֱלֹהֵינוּ,
5. There is none like our ruler   מִי כְּמוֹשִׁיעֵנוּ

Knowing the Prefixes
Fill in the missing translations.

1. אֲדוֹנֵינוּ means our holy one   לַאֲדוֹנֵינוּ means to our holy one
2. מַלְכֵּנוּ means _____   לְמַלְכֵּנוּ means _____
3. אֱלֹהֵינוּ means _____   לֵאלֹהֵינוּ means _____
4. מוֹשִׁיעֵנוּ means _____   לְמוֹשִׁיעֵנוּ means _____

The prefix לְ or לַ or before a word means _____.

Knowing the Suffixes
Fill in the missing translations.

1. מֶלֶךְ means ruler   מַלְכֵּנוּ means our ruler
2. אֱלֹהִים means _____   אֱלֹהֵינוּ means _____
3. אָדוֹן means _____   אֲדוֹנֵינוּ means _____
4. מוֹשִׁיעַ means _____   מוֹשִׁיעֵנוּ means _____

The suffix נוּ at the end of a word means _____.

Todah—Thank You

תּוֹדָה

    Back in Noah's day, besides trying to talk or pray to God, people felt a need to thank God in a physical way. When they survived a near-calamity (as Noah did) or celebrated a success (as Cain and Abel did), they brought a sacrifice to God. They took the best of their animals or crops, placed them on an altar, מִזְבֵּחַ, and burned them as an offering to show their devotion to God. By giving up something of value, they not only showed their love and respect, but also their trust that God would help them to prosper and replace those possessions.

    Later, during the reign of King Solomon, when the great Temple was built in Jerusalem, sacrifice became a part of the priestly duties. There are special laws in the Torah describing just how and when sacrifices were to be brought and offered.

    Today we have other ways of showing our thanks to God. We can do our best to observe the laws of the Torah, to do מִצְווֹת (like giving צְדָקָה and being kind to others), and of course we pray to God, telling our feelings directly.

    The history of the way we give thanks to God is explained in the prayer אֵין כֵּאלֹהֵינוּ which we sing to a lovely melody at Sabbath morning services. "There is none like our God," the prayer states. It goes on to say, "Let us give thanks to our God" because "You are our God."

יְבָרֶכְךָ יְיָ
May the Eternal Bless You

Knowing the Prayer Vocabulary

פָּנֶיךָ	towards you	יְבָרֶכְךָ	may He bless you
אֶל	to, towards	בֵּרֵךְ	he blessed
וִיחֻנֶּךָּ	and may He be gracious	וְיִשְׁמְרֶךָ	and may He watch over you
חֵן	grace, charm	שָׁמַר	He watched
נָשָׂא	he carried, lifted	יָאֵר	may he shine
וְיָשֵׂם	and may He grant you	הֵאִיר	he lit up
שָׂם	he placed	פָּנָיו	his face (presence)
לְךָ	to you	פָּנִים	face

Knowing the Words
Circle the correct Hebrew word.

1. may He bless you	בָּרוּךְ	שָׁלוֹם	יְבָרֶכְךָ	
2. he blessed	יָד	בֵּרֵךְ	פָּנָיו	
3. he carried, lifted	נָשָׂא	אֵלֶיךָ	יָאֵר	
4. and may He grant you	אֵלֶיךָ	וְיָשֵׂם	וְצִוָּנוּ	
5. he placed	שָׁם	קִדְּשָׁנוּ	בָּרוּךְ	
6. to you	לְךָ	אֲשֶׁר	אַתָּה	
7. his face	פָּנָיו	בָּשָׂר	הוּא	
8. face	אֱלֹהֵינוּ	פָּנִים	מֶלֶךְ	
9. towards you	אֵלֶיךָ	הוּא	הָעוֹלָם	
10. to, towards	בְּמִצְוֹתָיו	אֶת־הָעוֹלָם	אֶל	
11. and may He gracious to you	הוּא	וִיחֻנֶּךָּ	נוֹתֵן	
12. grace, charm	לְכָל	חֵן	בָּשָׂר	
13. he watched	שָׁמַר	וְיָשֵׂם	הַזָּן	
14. may He shine	יָאֵר	אַתָּה	יִשָּׂא	
15. and may He watch over you	וְיִשְׁמְרֶךָ	שָׁלוֹם	לֶחֶם	

All bow their heads as the rabbi asks God's blessing in the words of the ancient benediction used by the priests in the **Bet Hamikdash**.

May the Eternal bless you   יְבָרֶכְךָ יְיָ
    and may He watch over you   וְיִשְׁמְרֶךָ.
May the Eternal's presence shine towards you   יָאֵר יְיָ פָּנָיו אֵלֶיךָ
    and may He be gracious to you.   וִיחֻנֶּךָּ.
May the Eternal lift His presence towards you   יִשָּׂא יְיָ פָּנָיו אֵלֶיךָ,
    and may He grant you peace.   וְיָשֵׂם לְךָ שָׁלוֹם.

Knowing the Phrases
Draw a line from the Hebrew phrase to its English meaning.

1. may the Eternal lift his presence towards you   וְיִשְׁמְרֶךָ
2. and may He grant you peace   יִשָּׂא יְיָ פָּנָיו אֵלֶיךָ
3. may the Eternal bless you   וִיחֻנֶּךָּ
4. and may He watch over you   יָאֵר יְיָ פָּנָיו אֵלֶיךָ
5. may the Eternal's presence shine towards you   יְבָרֶכְךָ יְיָ
6. and may He be gracious to you.   וְיָשֵׂם לְךָ שָׁלוֹם

In Hebrew the word for "peace" is שָׁלוֹם. Shalom is so precious to us that it is both greeting and good-bye. Shalom is so precious that we pray for it a number of times each day. Here in the benediction, we ask God to grant peace for all peoples.

יְבָרֶכְךָ יְיָ וְיִשְׁמְרֶךָ!

יָאֵר יְיָ פָּנָיו אֵלֶיךָ וִיחֻנֶּךָ!

יִשָּׂא יְיָ פָּנָיו אֵלֶיךָ וְיָשֵׂם לְךָ שָׁלוֹם!

Knowing the Suffixes
Fill in the missing translations.

1. יְבָרֵךְ means he will bless   יְבָרֶכְךָ means he will bless you

2. יִשְׁמוֹר means _____   יִשְׁמְרֶךָ means _____

3. יָחֹן means _____   יְחֻנֶּךָ means _____

4. אֶל means _____   אֵלֶיךָ means _____

The suffix ךָ at the end of a word means _____.

שָׁלוֹם בַּיִת
Peace In the Household

A family is a lot like a football team. Each person in the family has a special place on the team. Mother and Father play the parts of coach and quarterback. They know all the rules of the game because they have played it a lot longer than anyone else on the team. The rest of the family play fullback, linemen, and ends.

When one of the children gets a good report card, the whole family team gains a lot of yards. When somebody doesn't obey the coach and makes a mistake, the whole team is put back. But if the player who did wrong says, "I'm sorry I did that. I won't do it again," the team goes ahead again toward the goal post. The goal for the family team is called שָׁלוֹם בַּיִת, which means "peace in the household." This does not mean there will never be arguments. But it does mean that all the members of the team can go into a huddle and talk things out.

It takes a lot of hard work for a football team to score a touchdown. But the whole team is filled with joy when it happens. It takes a lot of hard work for a family team to cross that goal line called שָׁלוֹם בַּיִת, too. But a family that works hard together like a good football team can cross the שָׁלוֹם בַּיִת goal line many times.

What Rules Should the Family Observe to Have שָׁלוֹם בַּיִת at home.

1. Everyone should. _____

2. No one should. _____

3. There should be. _____

4. There should not be. _____

The Hazzan

Public prayer is lead by the חַזָּן, one who has been appointed by the congregation as leader of its prayers before God, its שְׁלִיחַ־צִבּוּר. Usually, the חַזָּן introduces the prayer by singing the first few words. The congregation picks up the music and continues to chant the words of the entire section. The music of the חַזָּן adds beauty and variety to the words of the prayer.

The office of חַזָּן is, therefore, a very important and meaningful one in the ritual of prayer. It is also among the most ancient of all in our long history. The men who led their fellow exiles in Babylonia in the chanting of the Temple ritual were the first חַזָנִים. As the prayer service developed and became more complicated the office required that the חַזָּן be a trained professional. The חַזָּן is referred to by many titles:

Cantor of the Synagogue	חַזָּן
Master of Prayer	בַּעַל־תְּפִלָה
Messenger of the Congregation	שְׁלִיחַ־צִבּוּר

מַה־טֹבוּ אֹהָלֶיךָ
How Good are Your Tents

Knowing the Prayer Vocabulary

יַעֲקֹב	Jacob	מַה־טֹבוּ	how good
מִשְׁכְּנוֹתֶיךָ	your places of worship	טוֹב	good
מִשְׁכָּן	place of worship, sanctuary	אֹהָלֶיךָ	your tents
		אֹהֶל	tent

Knowing the Words
Circle the correct Hebrew word.

1. your tents — אֹהָלֶיךָ   עוֹלָם   עָשָׂה
2. your places of worship — הָאָרֶץ   מִשְׁכְּנֹתֶיךָ   אֹהֶל
3. tent — עוֹלָם   אֹהֶל   שַׁבָּת
4. Jacob — יַעֲקֹב   יִשְׂרָאֵל   קָדוֹשׁ
5. how good — יַעֲקֹב   שַׁבָּת   מַה־טֹבוּ
6. good — טוֹב   מִשְׁכְּנֹתֶיךָ   יִשְׂרָאֵל

The service often opens with this prayer, which praises the place where God is worshipped.

How good are your tents,   מַה־טֹּבוּ אֹהָלֶיךָ
    O Jacob,   יַעֲקֹב,
     your places of worship,   מִשְׁכְּנֹתֶיךָ
    O Israel.   יִשְׂרָאֵל.

Knowing the Phrases
Draw a line from the Hebrew phrase to its English meaning.

1. How good are your tents, O Jacob,   מִשְׁכְּנֹתֶיךָ יִשְׂרָאֵל
2. your places of worship, O Israel   מַה־טֹּבוּ אֹהָלֶיךָ יַעֲקֹב

Our Rabbis say that אוֹהָלֶיךָ "your tents" refers to synagogues, while מִשְׁכְּנוֹתֶיךָ "your places of worship" refers to religious schools where תּוֹרָה is taught.

$$\text{מַה־טֹּבוּ אֹהָלֶיךָ, יַעֲקֹב,}$$
$$\text{מִשְׁכְּנֹתֶיךָ יִשְׂרָאֵל.}$$

See page 160 for the complete מַה־טֹּבוּ

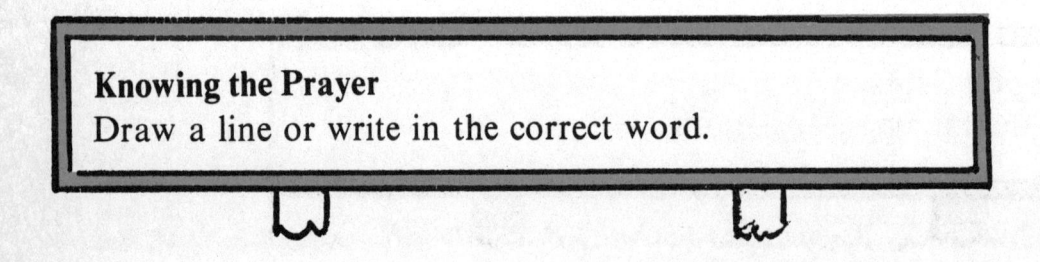

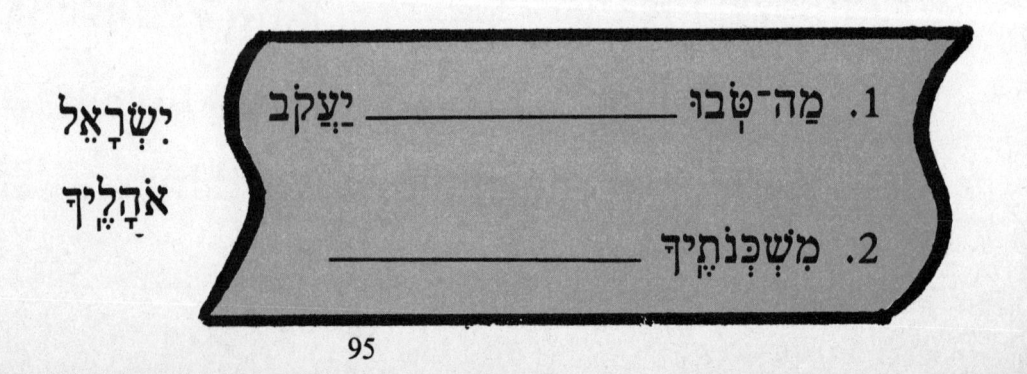

Knowing the Prayer
Draw a line or write in the correct word.

1. מַה־טֹּבוּ _____ יַעֲקֹב

2. מִשְׁכְּנֹתֶיךָ _____

יִשְׂרָאֵל
אֹהָלֶיךָ

Knowing the Answers
Write your answer to the question.

1. What is meant by the word "tents"?
   _____
   _____

2. What is meant by "places of worship"?
   _____
   _____

3. Is your home a "place of worship" or a "tent"?
   _____
   _____

Knowing the Suffixes
Fill in the missing translations.

1. אֹהָלִים means tents   אֹהָלֶיךָ means your tents
2. מִשְׁכְּנוֹת means _____   מִשְׁכְּנוֹתֶיךָ means _____
3. מִצְוֹת means _____   מִצְוֹתֶיךָ means _____

The suffix ךָ at the end of a word means _____ .

96

The Story of Balaam

Story Vocabulary

מֶלֶךְ בָּלָק	King Balak	בְּנֵי יִשְׂרָאֵל	Children of Israel
בִּלְעָם	Balaam	מֹשֶׁה	Moses
אָתוֹן	donkey	אֱמוֹרִי	Amorite
כְּנַעַן	Canaan	מוֹאָב	Moab
מַלְאָךְ	angel	מִצְרַיִם	Egypt

The years passed swiftly, and the small children of בְּנֵי יִשְׂרָאֵל, who had left מִצְרַיִם with מֹשֶׁה so long ago, had now grown to be fine strong men and women.

As the בְּנֵי יִשְׂרָאֵל neared the Land of כְּנַעַן, they came to the country of מוֹאָב.

The Moabites were ruled by a king whose name was בָּלָק, and he tried to form some plan for driving away the בְּנֵי יִשְׂרָאֵל from that region.

When Balak heard that the בְּנֵי יִשְׂרָאֵל were camped near the borders of his country, he said to himself:

"These people seem to cover the earth! But I shall not allow them to come into my kingdom! I must send messengers to the wise prophet and have him come here to curse these בְּנֵי יִשְׂרָאֵל!"

Now the name of this famous prophet, who lived many miles away from מוֹאָב, was בִּלְעָם.

People believed that whatever בִּלְעָם said was sure to come to pass; but they did not know that בִּלְעָם could only speak what God gave him to speak.

בִּלְעָם was very clever, and he also feared God, and did not want to do anything against the wishes of God. So when the messengers of מֶלֶךְ בָּלָק arrived and told the great prophet about the בְּנֵי יִשְׂרָאֵל, בִּלְעָם said:

"I cannot tell you right now whether I will go with you to מֶלֶךְ בָּלָק or not. You must remain here at my house overnight. I shall wait for God to tell me what to do."

That night, as בִּלְעָם lay on his bed, thinking about מֶלֶךְ בָּלָק and the בְּנֵי יִשְׂרָאֵל, he heard the voice of God say:

"Do not go with these men! Do not curse the בְּנֵי יִשְׂרָאֵל, for they are blessed!"

The next morning, בִּלְעָם said to the messengers:

"I am sorry, I cannot go with you. God has told me not to curse the בְּנֵי יִשְׂרָאֵל."

But when the messengers returned home and told מֶלֶךְ בָּלָק what בִּלְעָם had said, the king was very troubled.

"I will send princes with much silver to בִּלְעָם," he cried. "He must come to me and curse the בְּנֵי יִשְׂרָאֵל!"

When the princes arrived at the house of בִּלְעָם, bearing fine gifts and silver, Balaam said to them:

"Even if מֶלֶךְ בָּלָק gave me his whole house full of silver and gold, I still must do what God tells me to do. You must stay in my house overnight and I will listen to the voice of God."

That night, God said to בִּלְעָם:

"If the men ask you to go with them, rise up and go. But listen for the words I will tell you to say!"

And so the next morning, בִּלְעָם saddled his אָתוֹן and set out with the princes on the journey to מוֹאָב. But all of a sudden, the אָתוֹן began to act very strangely.

"You stupid אָתוֹן!" cried בִּלְעָם in great anger. But the אָתוֹן was not as stupid as בִּלְעָם thought. For she had seen something in the road that בִּלְעָם could not see. Twice, the אָתוֹן had seen a mighty מַלְאָךְ with a great shining sword, standing right in her path. A third time the אָתוֹן saw the מַלְאָךְ, and this time, the road was so narrow, there was no place for her to go, and she fell down under בִּלְעָם. Then בִּלְעָם was indeed angry. He hit the poor אָתוֹן with a stick. But God put words into the mouth of the אָתוֹן, and she said to בִּלְעָם:

"Why have you struck me? Have I not always obeyed you?"

בִּלְעָם was so astonished, he did not know what to think. But just then, God opened Balaam's eyes, so that he saw the מַלְאָךְ standing in the road. בִּלְעָם fell to his knees, for he knew this was a מַלְאָךְ of the Lord!

"Now, go with the men," cried the מַלְאָךְ, "but remember to say only what God tells you to say!"

מֶלֶךְ בָּלָק came to meet בִּלְעָם, and told him that he would give him much gold if he would curse the בְּנֵי יִשְׂרָאֵל. But בִּלְעָם answered:

"I cannot curse these people unless God tells me to!"

Then מֶלֶךְ בָּלָק took בִּלְעָם to a high mountain.

מֶלֶךְ בָּלָק waited and waited for the great prophet to put a curse upon these people who had camped outside his country.

But when בִּלְעָם finally opened his mouth to speak, בָּלָק heard him say these words:

"How can I curse these people whom God has not cursed!"

מֶלֶךְ בָּלָק was very angry. He took בִּלְעָם to another place and waited for him to speak. Once again בִּלְעָם opened his mouth, and spoke these words:

"God has commanded me to bless these people. For He has blessed them also. God brought the בְּנֵי יִשְׂרָאֵל out of מִצְרַיִם. These people shall rise up like a great lion and conquer the land!"

But מֶלֶךְ בָּלָק was not satisfied. He took בִּלְעָם to still another place, thinking surely this time the prophet would curse the בְּנֵי יִשְׂרָאֵל. But for the third time, בִּלְעָם opened his mouth, and spoke these words:

מַה־טֹּבוּ אֹהָלֶיךָ יַעֲקֹב "How good are your tents, O Jacob,

מִשְׁכְּנֹתֶיךָ יִשְׂרָאֵל. "The places where you live, O Israel.

When מֶלֶךְ בָּלָק heard this, he was so angry that he shouted:

"Go back to your home! I offered you all the gold and silver I possess to curse these בְּנֵי יִשְׂרָאֵל! You have done nothing but bless them! Get out of my sight!"

The words of בִּלְעָם were true. The בְּנֵי יִשְׂרָאֵל did rise up like a mighty lion. מֶלֶךְ בָּלָק found out what many people never learn: that you cannot buy the blessing of God with money. God gives his blessings freely, to all those who obey His laws!

The prophet בִּלְעָם standing on a Moabite hill was struck by the beauty of the Hebrew tents spread out in orderly rows.

He saw the colorful tribal emblems fluttering in the breeze. בִּלְעָם saw children playing and skipping as they went to their classes.

The prophet saw men and women proudly and energetically going about their daily duties.

בִּלְעָם saw a community of people living in peace and in harmony.

It was then that the spirit of God came upon him and he uttered these prophetic words, מַה־טֹּבוּ אֹהָלֶיךָ יַעֲקֹב
מִשְׁכְּנֹתֶיךָ יִשְׂרָאֵל.

You and Your Community

Have you ever moved into a new neighborhood? What were the first things you looked for? Did you try to find your temple and your school? Did you look for kids to play with? Perhaps you looked for the playground on your first day.

If you did these things, you were exploring your community.

A community is a place where people can get the things they need. Communities also have places where people live and work and play and learn and get help in case of trouble.

People all over the world live in communities. Communities come in different sizes, and the people there live in different ways.

1. What is the name of your community?
2. Who is the mayor of your community?
3. What is the emergency telephone number for the police department in your community?
4. What is the emergency telephone number for the fire department in your community?
5. What is the name of the hospital that is nearest to your home?
6. What is the telephone number for emergency ambulance service?
7. How do the kids in your community have fun?
8. What improvements would you like to make in your community?
9. How would you go about making your community a better place in which to live?

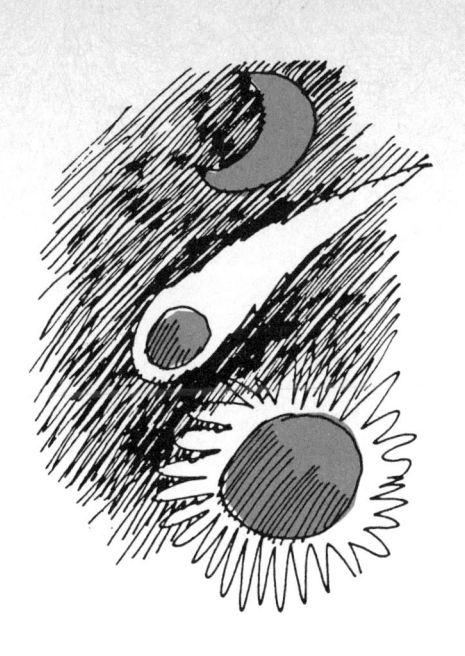

יוֹצֵר הַמְּאוֹרוֹת
Creator of Light

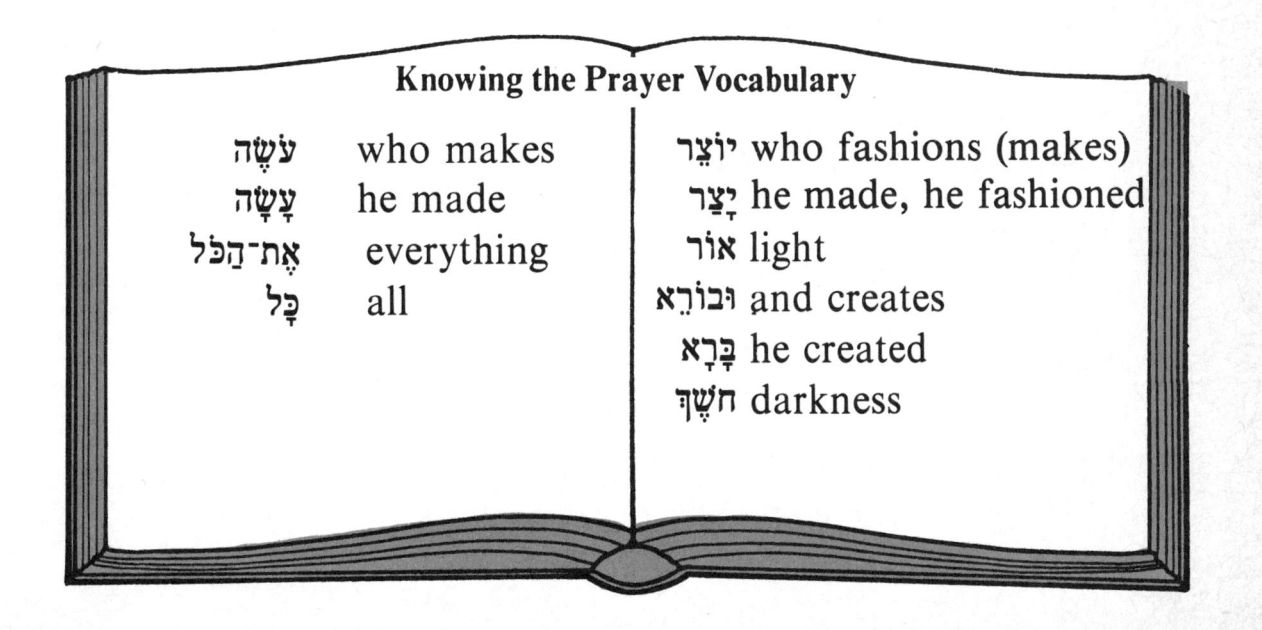

Knowing the Prayer Vocabulary

עֹשֶׂה	who makes	יוֹצֵר	who fashions (makes)
עָשָׂה	he made	יָצַר	he made, he fashioned
אֶת־הַכֹּל	everything	אוֹר	light
כֹּל	all	וּבוֹרֵא	and creates
		בָּרָא	he created
		חֹשֶׁךְ	darkness

Know the Words
Circle the correct Hebrew word.

1. darkness	הַכֹּל	וּבוֹרֵא	חֹשֶׁךְ	
2. who makes	אוֹר	עֹשֶׂה	יוֹצֵר	
3. light	אוֹר	עֹשֶׂה	וּבוֹרֵא	
4. he made	אוֹר	עֹשֶׂה	עָשָׂה	
5. and creates	וּבוֹרֵא	הָעוֹלָם	אֱלֹהֵינוּ	
6. he created	חֹשֶׁךְ	בָּרָא	בָּרוּךְ	
7. everything	אֶת־הַכֹּל	הָעוֹלָם	שָׁלוֹם	
8. who fashions (makes)	שָׁלוֹם	יוֹצֵר	הַזָּן	
9. he fashioned	יָצַר	חֹשֶׁךְ	בּוֹרֵא	
10. darkness	חֹשֶׁךְ	וּבוֹרֵא	יוֹצֵר	

The יוֹצֵר הַמְּאוֹרוֹת ("Creator of Light") prayer thanks God for creating light and filling the world with so many wonderful things.

Blessed are You, Eternal,	בָּרוּךְ אַתָּה יְיָ,
our God, ruler of the world	אֱלֹהֵינוּ מֶלֶךְ הָעוֹלָם,
who fashions light,	יוֹצֵר אוֹר
and creates darkness,	וּבוֹרֵא חֹשֶׁךְ,
who makes peace,	עֹשֶׂה שָׁלוֹם,
and creates everything.	וּבוֹרֵא אֶת־הַכֹּל.

Knowing the Phrases
Draw a line from the Hebrew phrase to its English meaning.

1. who makes peace	יוֹצֵר אוֹר
2. and creates everything.	עֹשֶׂה שָׁלוֹם
3. who fashions light	וּבוֹרֵא חֹשֶׁךְ
4. and creates darkness,	וּבוֹרֵא אֶת־הַכֹּל

All the universe is controlled by God. It is God's will that the sun rises in the morning and sets at night.

בָּרוּךְ אַתָּה יְיָ, אֱלֹהֵינוּ מֶלֶךְ הָעוֹלָם, יוֹצֵר אוֹר וּבוֹרֵא חֹשֶׁךְ, עֹשֶׂה שָׁלוֹם, וּבוֹרֵא אֶת הַכֹּל.

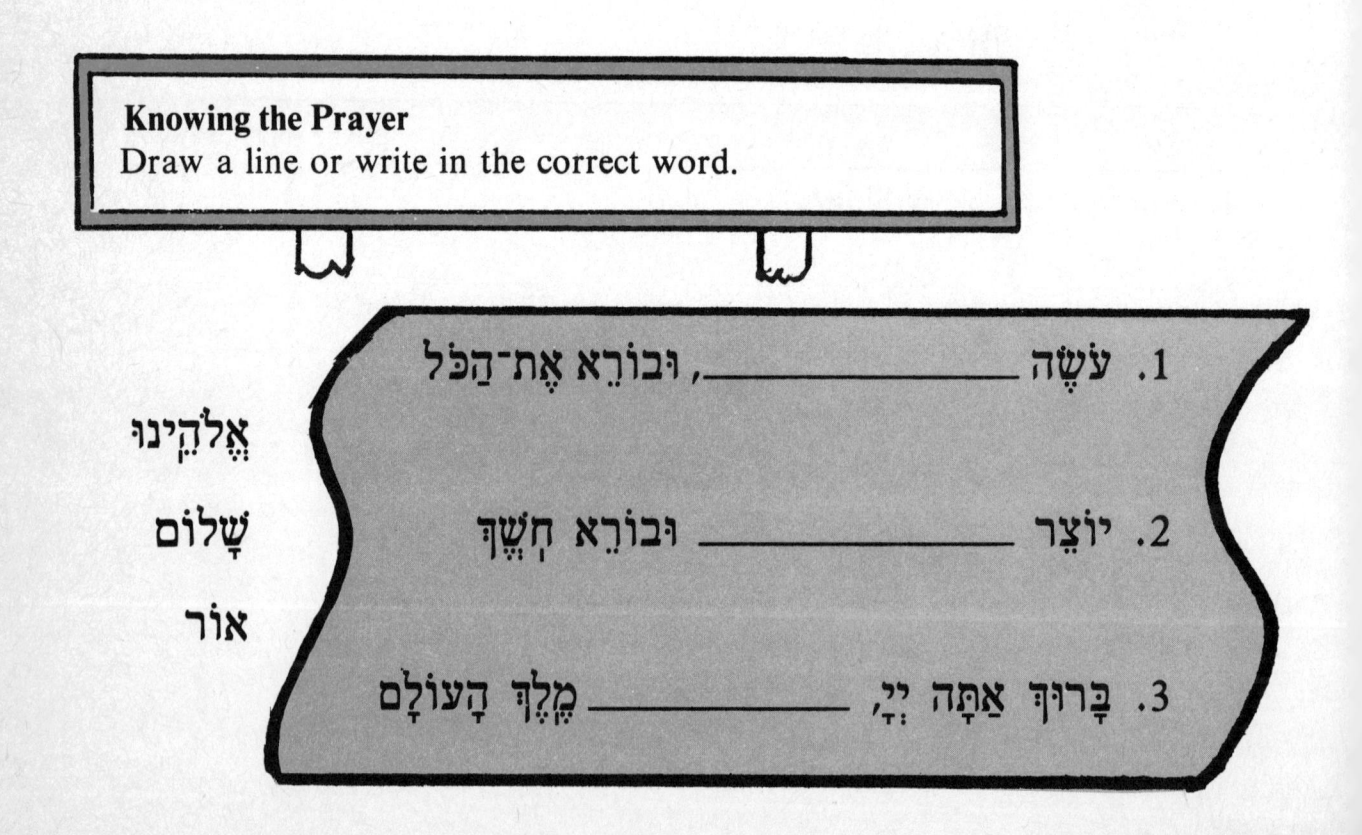

Knowing the Prayer
Draw a line or write in the correct word.

1. עֹשֶׂה _____, וּבוֹרֵא אֶת־הַכֹּל

אֱלֹהֵינוּ

2. יוֹצֵר _____ וּבוֹרֵא חֹשֶׁךְ

שָׁלוֹם

אוֹר

3. בָּרוּךְ אַתָּה יְיָ, _____ מֶלֶךְ הָעוֹלָם

Knowing the Answers
Write your answer to the questions.

1. What is meant by ruler of the world?

2. Who created light and darkness?

3. Who is the maker of peace?

4. Who created everything?

The Miracle of Light

The Bible tells us that when God was creating the world, God made the sun, moon, and stars on the fourth day. Next, on the fifth and sixth day, God made living things.

There is a very important reason why God made the world in this way. The sun and stars give light—and the moon gives light reflected from the sun. Almost every living thing needs light so that it can live and grow.

People and animals need light so they can see each other. Imagine what the world would be like without light! Hold your hand over your eyes so that you cannot see anything at all. This is how the whole world would be without light. You could not see where you were going. You could not see your family or friends and they could not see you. The world would be impossible to live in without light.

What Do You Think?

1. Why do plants need light to grow?
2. Why do people need sunlight to be healthy?
3. Why do people like to go to the beach?
4. How do you feel in a room with very dim lights?
5. Why are decorations for holidays and parties always made of bright colors?
6. How do you feel on a rainy day? Why?
7. How do you feel on a sunny day? Why

The Siddur and You

Only God can create something from nothing. However, we human beings are very intelligent and smart creatures. We can invent new machines, write books, paint beautiful pictures, and do many things to make our lives happier, safer, and more interesting. We have the ability to learn to do new things.

Name some things that you cannot do that you would like to learn.

Imagine that this is the year 2000. What changes would you like to see? What new inventions would you like to see?

Name some things that you have never done that you would like to try to do.

קְדוּשָׁה
Sanctification

Knowing the Prayer Vocabulary

כָּל הָאָרֶץ	all the earth	קָדוֹשׁ	holy
אֶרֶץ	earth, land	צְבָאוֹת	hosts
כְּבוֹדוֹ	his glory	מְלֹא	is full of
כָּבוֹד	glory	מָלֵא	he filled

Knowing the Words
Circle the correct Hebrew word.

1. hosts, armies	צְבָאוֹת	מְלֹא	כְּבוֹדוֹ
2. is full of	קָדוֹשׁ	צְבָאוֹת	מְלֹא
3. all the earth	הָעוֹלָם	כָּל־הָאָרֶץ	קָדוֹשׁ
4. his glory	הָאָרֶץ	מְלֹא	כְּבוֹדוֹ
5. holy	קָדוֹשׁ	צְבָאוֹת	כָּל־הָאָרֶץ

109

The קְדוּשָׁה (Sanctification) describes the feeling of awe we experience when thinking about God's holiness.

"Holy, holy, holy   קָדוֹשׁ קָדוֹשׁ קָדוֹשׁ

is the God of hosts.   יְיָ צְבָאוֹת,

All the earth is full   מְלֹא כָל־הָאָרֶץ

of His (God's) glory."   כְּבוֹדוֹ.

Knowing the Phrases
Draw a line from the Hebrew phrase to its English meaning.

1. all the earth is full   קָדוֹשׁ קָדוֹשׁ קָדוֹשׁ
2. Holy, holy, holy   מְלֹא כָל־הָאָרֶץ
3. is the God of Hosts   יְיָ צְבָאוֹת

Knowing the Suffixes
Fill in the missing translations.

1. חֶסֶד means kindness   חַסְדוֹ means his kindness
2. טוֹב means _____   טוּבוֹ means _____
3. כָּבוֹד means _____   כְּבוֹדוֹ means _____

The suffix וֹ at the end of a word means _____

These words come from the prophet Isaiah. The word קָדוֹשׁ is said three times to teach us three things: (1) God is holy in the highest heaven, (2) God is holy on earth, which was created with heavenly power, and (3) God will be holy forever and ever.

$$\text{קָדוֹשׁ קָדוֹשׁ קָדוֹשׁ יְיָ צְבָאוֹת מְלֹא כָל הָאָרֶץ כְּבוֹדוֹ.}$$

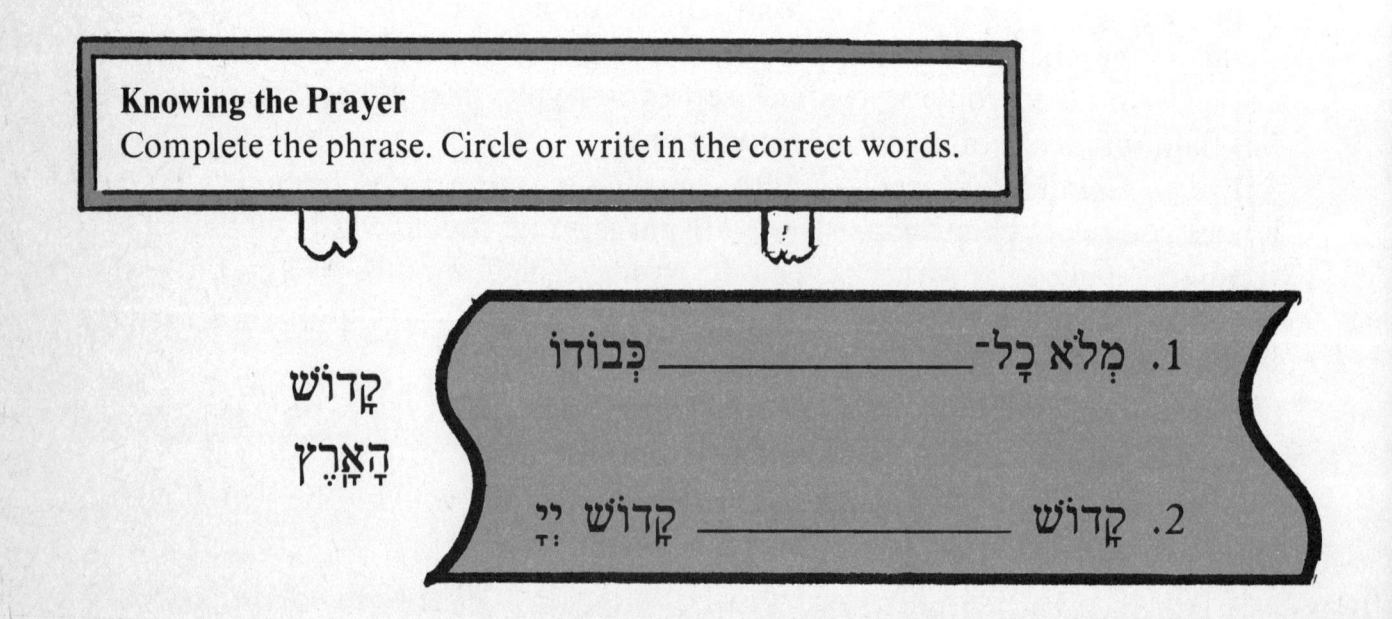

Knowing the Prayer
Complete the phrase. Circle or write in the correct words.

1. מְלֹא כָל־ _____ כְּבוֹדוֹ

2. קָדוֹשׁ _____ קָדוֹשׁ יְיָ

קָדוֹשׁ
הָאָרֶץ

יֵצֶר הָרַע יֵצֶר טוֹב
Choosing Between Good and Evil

God made us free. God gave us free will to choose between doing good or evil.

You may find that it's hard to be good. You may find that it's fun to say something mean to someone instead of saying something nice. Our rabbis tell us that's because every person in the world is born with a good side and a bad side and the freedom to choose between them. The good side is called יֵצֶר הַטוֹב and the bad side יֵצֶר הָרַע. The טוֹב side says, "Be good, be kind," but the רַע says, "Be selfish, be mean!" And so the טוֹב and רַע are always fighting, each one trying to have its own way.

But it's up to *you* to choose. Many times you have to choose between something wrong that seems like fun and something right that seems like a real "drag." And the people who are close to you—your family, your friends—will have an important influence on your choice.

Even a friend might lead you into choosing the יֵצֶר הָרַע. "Everybody's doing it" or "You're not chicken, are you?" are phrases that should warn you that your friend is trying to convince you to do wrong. That's why it's so important to choose your friends carefully. A good friend will help you to choose right, and a bad friend will lead you to do wrong.

Sometimes the choice between good and evil may not really be clear to you. Suppose your best friend told you he had to pass an important test or he would fail the course and have to go to summer school. He wouldn't be able to go to summer camp, and his family would be awfully mad! If he wanted you to give

him the test answers, what would you do? That would be a good problem to discuss with someone whose opinion you can trust—maybe your mother or father. They might suggest that you help your ofriend by tutoring him *before* the exam so that he would be able to pass by himself. He would feel better if he passed honestly, too.

That's the big difference between טוֹב and רַע. When you listen to the טוֹב and do the right thing, you feel great! But if you do what the רַע says, you feel guilty and find that you don't like yourself. The choice is up to you!

What Do You Think?
Write the word טוֹב or רַע next to each picture.

הוֹצָאַת הַתּוֹרָה
The Removal of the Torah From the Ark

Knowing the Prayer Vocabulary

יְרוּשָׁלַיִם	Jerusalem	מִצִּיוֹן	from Zion
שֶׁנָּתַן	who gave	צִיוֹן	Zion
לְעַמּוֹ	to his people	תֵּצֵא	will go forth
עַם	people, nation	יָצָא	he went forth
בִּקְדֻשָּׁתוֹ	in all its holiness	וּדְבַר	and (the) word
קְדֻשָּׁה	holiness	דָּבָר	word, thing
		מִירוּשָׁלַיִם	from Jerusalem

Knowing the Words
Circle the correct Hebrew word.

1. will go forth	יִשְׂרָאֵל	שָׁלוֹם	תֵּצֵא
2. who gave	הוּא	תּוֹרָה	שֶׁנָּתַן
3. from Zion	מִצִּיּוֹן	בָּרְכוּ	לְעוֹלָם
4. people, nation	בִּקְדֻשָׁתוֹ	הָעוֹלָם	עַם
5. in all its holiness	בִּקְדֻשָׁתוֹ	מֶלֶךְ	יִשְׂרָאֵל
6. he went forth	יָצָא	אַתָּה	לְעוֹלָם
7. and (the) word	וּדְבַר	הוּא	וּדְבַר

The city of Jerusalem is very old, dating back to the time of King David, who made it the capital of Israel. It has been conquered and retaken, destroyed and rebuilt more often than any city in the world. All through Persian, Moslem, Mamluk, Tartar, and Turkish control, Jewish continued to live in Jerusalem despite the many hardships.
The Crusaders burned all Jews found in the city in 1099. Nevertheless, other Jews came to replace them.
 In 1917, the Turks were driven out of the Holy Land by General Allenby. When the State of Israel was established in 1948, Jerusalem was a divided city. Jordan had captured the Old City of Jerusalem. However, in 1967, during the Six-Day War, Israel recaptured the Old City. Today, Jerusalem is the undivided capital of Israel.

As the Torah is taken from the ark, we sing this prayer. This prayer comes from the Book of Isaiah. It is a famous verse, telling us that one day the תּוֹרָה, the teachings of Judaism, will come forth from Zion and the Word of God will come forth from Jerusalem. In other words, we shall one day be established in the Land of Israel and spread our great ideas and ideals throughout the world.

For from Zion the Torah will go forth,   כִּי מִצִיוֹן תֵּצֵא תוֹרָה

    and the word of the Eternal from Jerusalem.   וּדְבַר־יְיָ מִירוּשָׁלָיִם:

Blessed be the One who gave the Torah,   בָּרוּךְ שֶׁנָּתַן תּוֹרָה

    to His people Israel   לְעַמּוֹ יִשְׂרָאֵל

    in all its holiness   בִּקְדֻשָּׁתוֹ.

Knowing the Phrases
Draw a line from the Hebrew phrase to its English meaning.

1. Blessed is the One who gave the Torah   כִּי מִצִיוֹן תֵּצֵא תוֹרָה
2. to his people Israel   וּדְבַר־יְיָ מִירוּשָׁלָיִם
3. in all its holiness   בָּרוּךְ שֶׁנָּתַן תּוֹרָה
4. For from Zion will go forth the Torah   לְעַמּוֹ יִשְׂרָאֵל
5. and the word of the Eternal from Jerusalem   בִּקְדֻשָּׁתוֹ

The first verse in this prayer comes from the Book of Isaiah. Then, the prophet continues, "They shall beat their swords into plough shares, and their spears into pruning hooks. Nation shall not lift up sword against nation, neither shall they learn war anymore."

כִּי מִצִּיּוֹן תֵּצֵא תוֹרָה,
וּדְבַר יְיָ מִירוּשָׁלָיִם.

בָּרוּךְ, שֶׁנָּתַן תּוֹרָה לְעַמּוֹ יִשְׂרָאֵל בִּקְדֻשָּׁתוֹ.

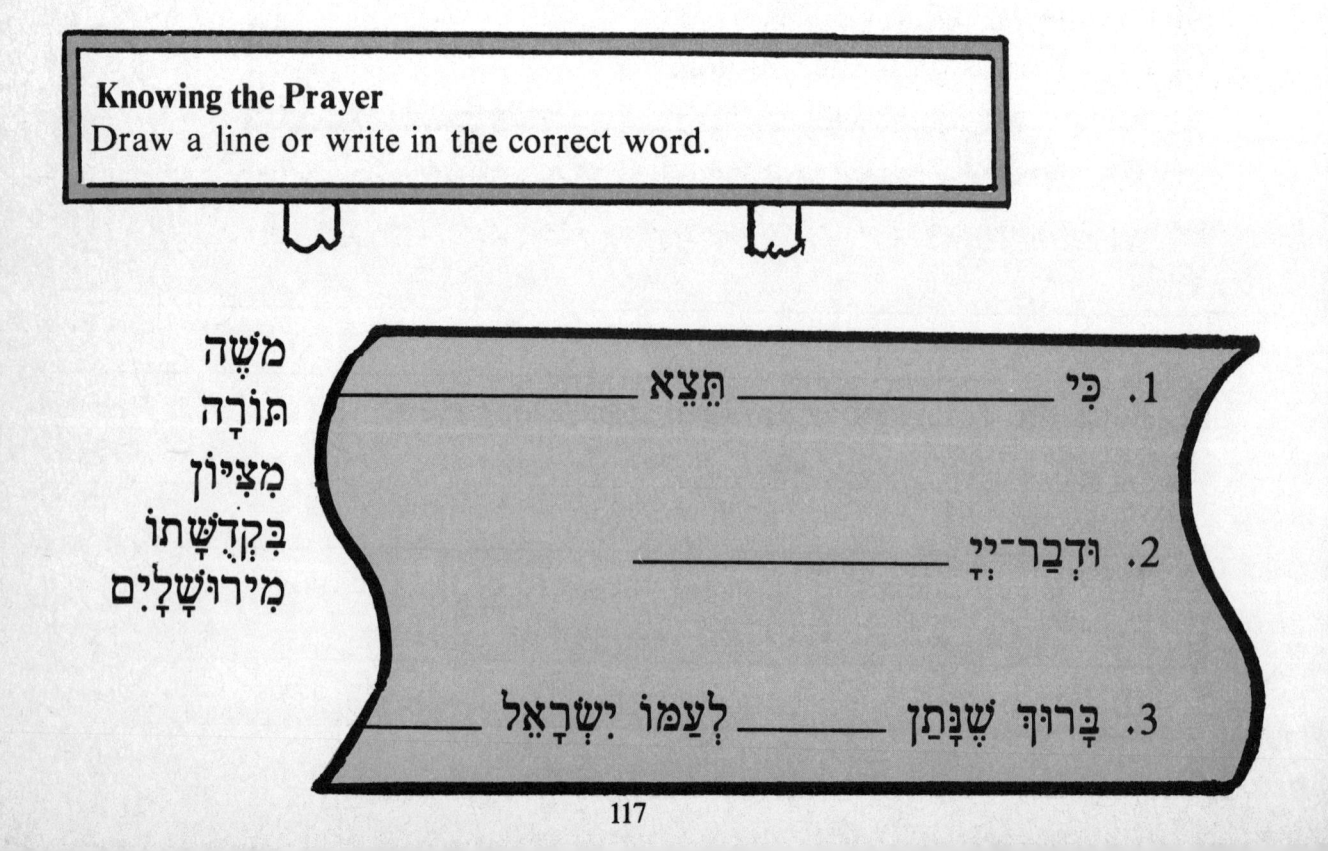

Knowing the Prayer
Draw a line or write in the correct word.

מֹשֶׁה
תּוֹרָה
מִצִּיּוֹן
בִּקְדֻשָּׁתוֹ
מִירוּשָׁלָיִם

1. כִּי _____ תֵּצֵא _____

2. וּדְבַר־יְיָ _____

3. בָּרוּךְ שֶׁנָּתַן _____ לְעַמּוֹ יִשְׂרָאֵל _____

117

Knowing the Prefixes
Fill in the missing translations.

1. צִיּוֹן means Zion   מִצִּיּוֹן means from Zion

2. יְרוּשָׁלַיִם means _____   מִירוּשָׁלַיִם means _____

3. יִשְׂרָאֵל means _____   מִיִּשְׂרָאֵל means _____

4. מֹשֶׁה means _____   מִמֹּשֶׁה means _____

The prefix מִ before a word means _____.

Knowing the Answers
Write the answer to the questions.

1. Where is Zion?
_____
_____

2. Does the Torah today go forth from Zion? How?
_____
_____

3. Why is Jerusalem the place for the word of the Eternal?
_____
_____

סֵדֶר קְרִיאַת הַתּוֹרָה לְשַׁבָּת וּלְיוֹם טוֹב
Order of Reading the Torah For Sabbaths and Festivals

קְרִיאַת הַתּוֹרָה, the reading of the תּוֹרָה in the synagogue, is a most important part of the service on Sabbaths and holidays.

This custom began with Ezra the Scribe, who revived religious life in ancient Palestine.

Each year we complete the reading of the entire תּוֹרָה. We divide the תּוֹרָה reading into fifty-four סְדְרוֹת, or portions.

When we finish the סְדְרָה, we read the הַפְטָרָה, a portion from one of the books of the Prophets (נְבִיאִים). Usually the הַפְטָרָה has a connection with the סְדְרָה read on that day.

Eight men in all are called to the reading (קְרִיאָה). The first is a כֹּהֵן, the second is a לֵוִי, and the rest are יִשְׂרָאֵל. The last man to be called to the תּוֹרָה is the מַפְטִיר, which means "the one who finishes." He also chants the הַפְטָרָה. On festivals we have special תּוֹרָה readings.

It is a wonderful thing that the study of the תּוֹרָה and the books of the great Prophets of Israel are part of our synagogue service. Our rabbis say that the very world rests on the study of the תּוֹרָה.

בָּרְכוּ אֶת־יְיָ
Blessed is the Eternal

Knowing the Prayer Vocabulary

לְעוֹלָם וָעֶד	forever and ever	בָּרְכוּ	blessed
עוֹלָם	world, ever	בֵּרַךְ	he blessed
וָעֶד	and ever	הַמְבֹרָךְ	who is blessed

Knowing the Prayer

Complete the phrase. Circle or write in the correct words.

1. and ever	וָעֶד	הַמְבֹרָךְ	לְעוֹלָם
2. world, ever	עוֹלָם	בָּרְכוּ	הַמְבֹרָךְ
3. blessed	אֶת־יְיָ	בָּרְכוּ	בָּרוּךְ
4. forever and ever	הַמְבֹרָךְ	הָאָרֶץ	לְעוֹלָם וָעֶד
5. he blessed	מִן	בֵּרַךְ	מֶלֶךְ
6. who is blessed	לֶחֶם	אֱלֹהֵינוּ	הַמְבֹרָךְ
7. he blessed	בֵּרַךְ	הַמּוֹצִיא	בָּרְכוּ

The בָּרְכוּ is also a call to worship. It is the signal to the congregation that in a short while the most important of all our prayers, the שְׁמַע, will begin. The בָּרְכוּ was even used in the days of the Holy Temple in Jerusalem. In the early morning, just as soon as the sun arose in the sky, a כֹּהֵן (priest) would call out, בָּרְכוּ אֶת יְיָ הַמְבֹרָךְ. And all who could would hear him answer, בָּרוּךְ יְיָ הַמְבֹרָךְ לְעוֹלָם וָעֶד.

Blessed is the Eternal	בָּרְכוּ אֶת־יְיָ
who is blessed.	הַמְבֹרָךְ.
Blessed is the Eternal	בָּרוּךְ יְיָ
who is blessed	הַמְבֹרָךְ
forever and ever.	לְעוֹלָם וָעֶד.

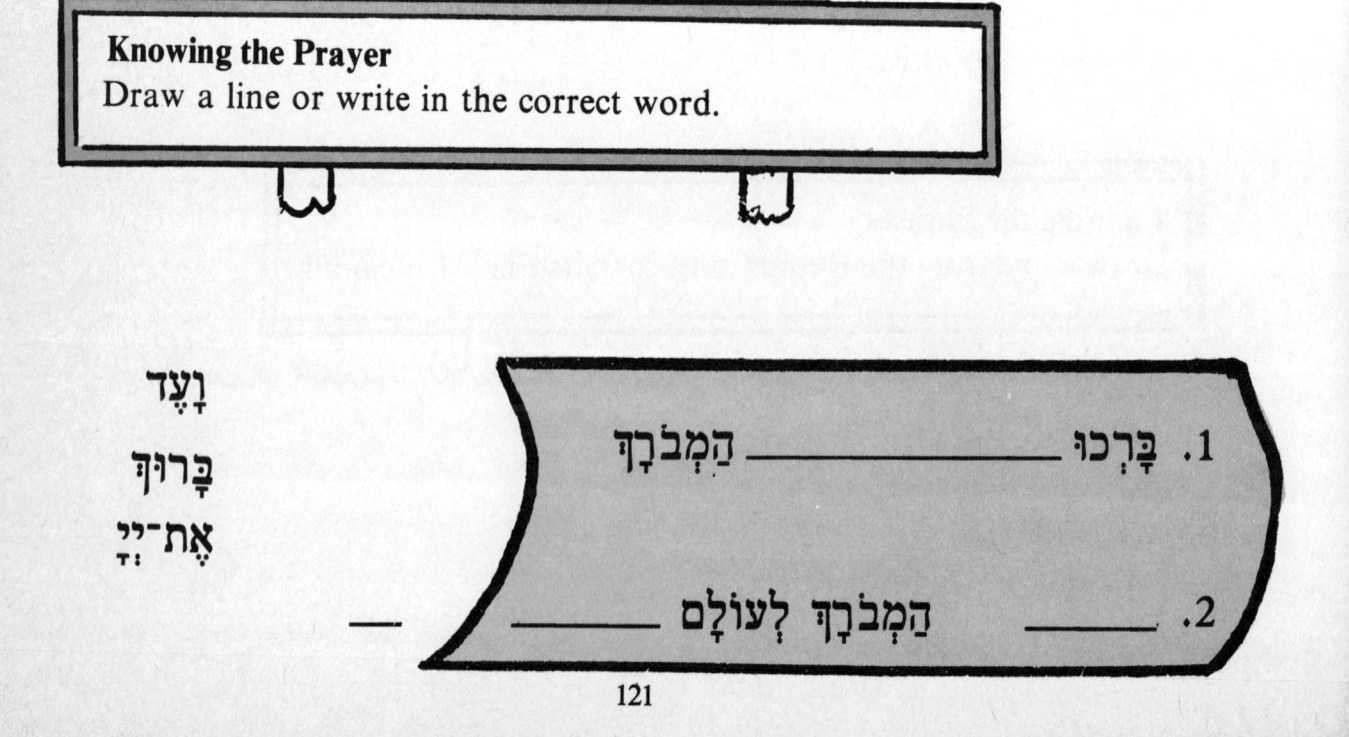

Knowing the Prayer
Draw a line or write in the correct word.

וָעֶד

בָּרוּךְ

אֶת־יְיָ

1. בָּרְכוּ _____ הַמְבֹרָךְ

2. _____ _____ הַמְבֹרָךְ לְעוֹלָם _____

The congregant who is honored with an עֲלִיָה comes up to the בִּימָה. The reader shows the honoree the place in the תּוֹרָה where the reading will begin. The congregant touches the place with the טַלִית. Then, taking hold of the two rollers of the תּוֹרָה, and with the תּוֹרָה opened, recites the blessing: בָּרְכוּ, the call to worship. The congregation responds, בָּרוּךְ יְיָ הַמְבֹרָךְ לְעוֹלָם וָעֶד. The honoree repeats בָּרוּךְ יְיָ הַמְבֹרָךְ לְעוֹלָם וָעֶד

The honoree who is honored with an עֲלִיָה recites:

בָּרְכוּ אֶת־יְיָ הַמְבֹרָךְ:

The congregation recites:

בָּרוּךְ יְיָ הַמְבֹרָךְ לְעוֹלָם וָעֶד:

The honoree repeats:

בָּרוּךְ יְיָ הַמְבֹרָךְ לְעוֹלָם וָעֶד:

Knowing the Phrases
Draw a line from the Hebrew phrase to its English meaning.

1. Blessed is the Eternal   לְעוֹלָם וָעֶד

2. forever and ever   בָּרוּךְ יְיָ הַמְבֹרָךְ

Knowing the Answers
Write your answer to each of the questions.

1. Why does God deserve praise?
   _____
   _____

2. How do we praise God?
   _____
   _____

3. Why does God want our praise?
   _____
   _____

4. When was the בָּרְכוּ recited in the days of the Holy Temple?
   _____
   _____

תּוֹרָה
The Torah

When we say "Bible," we often mean the תּוֹרָה, the Five Books of Moses. These five holy books tell the ancient history of the Jewish people from the creation of the world up to the time we reached the Promised Land of Israel. They describe our customs and ceremonies, including the 613 מִצְווֹת (commandments).

The Hebrew name for each of the five books is taken from the first meaningful word in that book. The first book, בְּרֵאשִׁית, called *Genesis* in English, tells the story of the creation of the world and tells about our ancestors.

The second book שְׁמוֹת called *Exodus* in English, describes the life of the Jews in Egypt and tells how they left Egypt and received the Ten Commandments at Mount Sinai. The third book, וַיִּקְרָא, called *Leviticus* in English, lists the laws and work of the כֹּהֲנִים (priests) in the ancient Temple in Jerusalem and lists laws. בַּמִּדְבָּר, the fourth book, called *Numbers* in English, tells the story of the wanderings of the Children of Israel for forty years in the desert. דְּבָרִים, or *Deuteronomy* in English, reviews the laws and commandments set down in the rest of the Torah.

Because the Torah contains so much beauty and wisdom in so short a space, it is difficult to know or understand all that the Torah has to teach us. Therefore, we read and study the Torah all the time. The Torah is read aloud in the synagogue three times a week. Each Sabbath a new portion, or סְדְרָה, of the Torah is chanted. When we read the last portion on the holiday of שִׂמְחַת תּוֹרָה, "Rejoicing with the Torah," we immediately begin again by reading the very first portion of the Torah too. This is our way of showing that you can never really finish the study of the Torah. There is always something new to be learned from it.

The Torah that we read in the synagogue is a scroll that has been handwritten by a scribe on parchment, not paper. It has no punctuation marks and no vowels, so you must know the Torah well before you can read it aloud in the synagogue. The Torah scrolls are kept in the אֲרוֹן הַקֹּדֶשׁ, Holy Ark.

נוֹתֵן הַתּוֹרָה
Giver of the Torah

Knowing the Prayer Vocabulary

נָתַן	he gave	בָּחַר	he chose
תּוֹרָתוֹ	His Torah	בָּנוּ	us
תּוֹרָה	Torah	מִכָּל	from all
נוֹתֵן	giver	הָעַמִּים	the nations
נָתַן	he gave	עַם	nation
לָנוּ	us	וְנָתַן	and gave

Knowing the Words
Circle the correct Hebrew word.

1. giver	נוֹתֵן	אֲשֶׁר	בָּרוּךְ
2. us	בָּנוּ	בָּחַר	מִכָּל
3. the nations	הָעַמִּים	הָעוֹלָם	אֱלֹהֵינוּ
4. nation	תּוֹרָתוֹ	עַם	שַׁבָּת
5. and gave	בְּחֶסֶד	בְּחֵן	וְנָתַן
6. he chose	וְצִוָּנוּ	בָּחַר	נוֹתֵן
7. us	הַזָּן	וּבְרַחֲמִים	לָנוּ
8. from all	מִכָּל	מֶלֶךְ	לֶחֶם
9. he gave	בְּטוּבוֹ	בָּשָׂר	נָתַן
10. His Torah	כֻּלּוֹ	תּוֹרָתוֹ	לְהַדְלִיק
11. Torah	תּוֹרָה	אַתָּה	לָנוּ

> When we read the Torah we use a special chant based on musical notes. These notes are called the "Trop" or *Ta'ame N'ginah*. According to tradition, we read this system in order to read the Scriptures as they were read in the days of Ezra and Nehemiah.

This is the first of the two Torah blessings. The prayer says that God has chosen us from all the nations. This means that we have more duties and responsibilities than other people.

How did God choose us from all the nations? By giving us the Torah. God gave us the Torah on Mount Sinai. The Torah is now in our charge. It is up to us to be "a light to the nations" by observing the laws of the Torah.

Blessed are You, Eternal,   בָּרוּךְ אַתָּה יְיָ,
    our God, ruler of the world,   אֱלֹהֵינוּ מֶלֶךְ הָעוֹלָם,
    who chose us   אֲשֶׁר בָּחַר־בָּנוּ
    from all the nations   מִכָּל־הָעַמִּים,
    and gave us His Torah.   וְנָתַן לָנוּ אֶת־תּוֹרָתוֹ.

Blessed is the Eternal,   בָּרוּךְ אַתָּה יְיָ,
    giver of the Torah.   נוֹתֵן הַתּוֹרָה.

Knowing the Phrases
Draw a line from the Hebrew phrase to its English meaning.

1. giver of the Torah   וְנָתַן לָנוּ אֶת־תּוֹרָתוֹ

2. who chose us   נוֹתֵן הַתּוֹרָה

3. and gave us His Torah   אֲשֶׁר בָּחַר בָּנוּ

The congregant who is honored with an עֲלִיָה comes up to the בִּימָה. The reader shows the honoree the place in the תּוֹרָה where the reading will begin. The congregant touches the place with the טַלִית. Then, taking hold of the two rollers of the תּוֹרָה, and with the תּוֹרָה opened, recites the blessing: בָּרְכוּ, the call to worship. The congregation responds, בָּרוּךְ יְיָ הַמְבֹרָךְ לְעוֹלָם וָעֶד. The honoree repeats בָּרוּךְ יְיָ הַמְבֹרָךְ לְעוֹלָם וָעֶד and then recites this blessing.

בָּרוּךְ אַתָּה יְיָ, אֱלֹהֵינוּ מֶלֶךְ הָעוֹלָם, אֲשֶׁר בָּחַר בָּנוּ מִכָּל הָעַמִּים, וְנָתַן לָנוּ אֶת תּוֹרָתוֹ.
בָּרוּךְ אַתָּה יְיָ, נוֹתֵן הַתּוֹרָה.

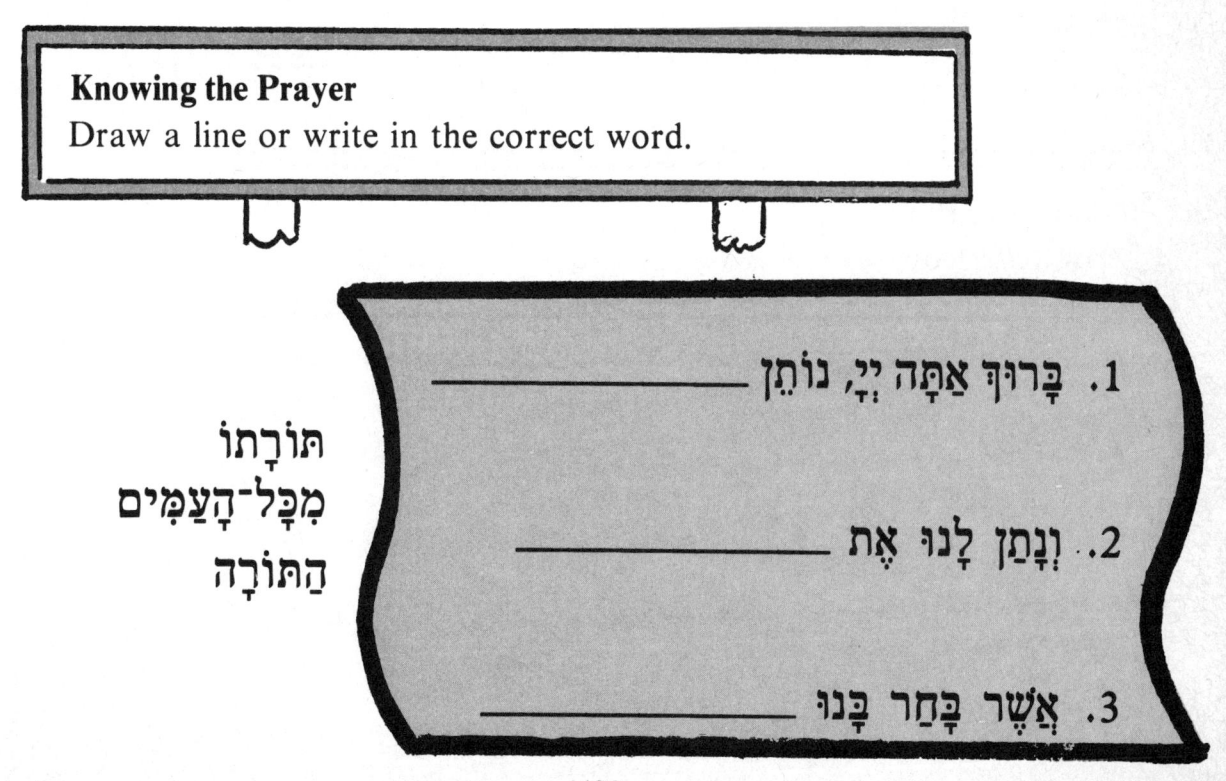

Knowing the Prayer
Draw a line or write in the correct word.

1. בָּרוּךְ אַתָּה יְיָ, נוֹתֵן _____

2. וְנָתַן לָנוּ אֶת _____

3. אֲשֶׁר בָּחַר בָּנוּ _____

תּוֹרָתוֹ
מִכָּל־הָעַמִּים
הַתּוֹרָה

Knowing the Suffixes
Fill in the missing translations.

1. תּוֹרָה means Torah   תּוֹרָתוֹ means his Torah
2. עוֹלָם means _____   עוֹלָמוֹ means _____
3. עַם means _____   עַמּוֹ means _____

The suffix וֹ at the end of a word means _____.

Knowing the Suffixes
Fill in the missing translations.

1. יוֹם means day   יָמִים means days
2. דֶּרֶךְ means _____   דְּרָכִים means _____
3. עַם means _____   עַמִּים means _____

The suffix ים at the end of a word means _____

Knowing the Ideas
Draw a line from the Hebrew phrase to the correct idea.

1. God gave the Torah to the Jews.   אֲשֶׁר בָּחַר־בָּנוּ מִכָּל־הָעַמִּים
2. God chose us   בָּרוּךְ אַתָּה יְיָ, נוֹתֵן הַתּוֹרָה

The Bible

The word *Bible* means "book." But the Bible is really a collection of books all in one book. It is a "library" of books holy to our people.

Our most cherished possession, the Bible, has been translated from Hebrew into over a thousand languages. It continues today, as in ages past, to help people lead a righteous life. The Bible tells us that there is One God; it teaches us to honor our parents; it urges us to tell only the truth. The Bible contains the world's most wonderful stories—of heroic people like Moses, Joshua, Deborah, and Samson; of important events like the Flood and the Exodus; of stirring prophecies like those of Isaiah and Jeremiah.

For us, the Bible—especially the Torah—has been the very center of Jewish spiritual life. Study it over and over again, said the Rabbis, for all knowledge and wisdom may be found in it.

The Bible consists of twenty-four books divided into three sections: The תּוֹרָה, the נְבִיאִים, and the כְּתוּבִים.

The *Torah* consists of the first five books of the Bible, called the Five Books of Moses.

The names of the Five Books of Moses in Hebrew are:

בְּרֵאשִׁית, שְׁמוֹת, וַיִּקְרָא, בַּמִּדְבָּר, דְּבָרִים

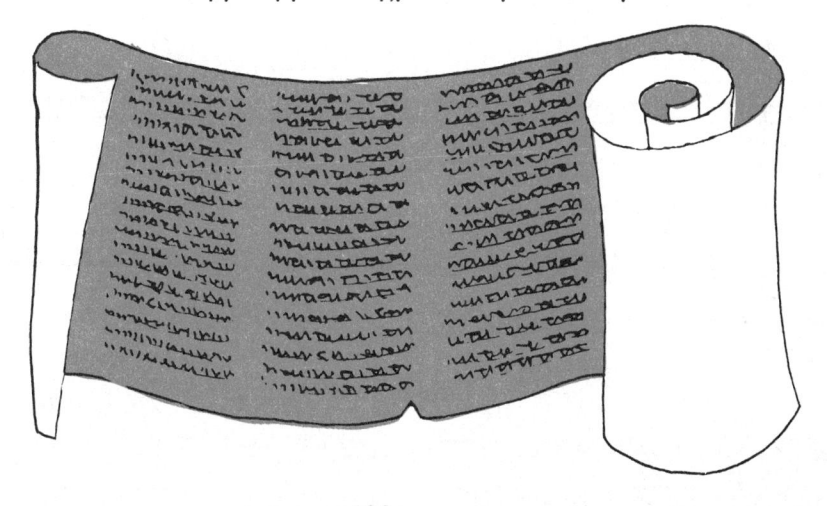

תּוֹרַת אֱמֶת
The Torah of Truth

Knowing the Prayer Vocabulary

חַיִּים	life	נָתַן	he gave
נָטַע	he planted	לָנוּ	to us
בְּתוֹכֵנוּ	in our midst	תּוֹרַת	the Torah of
תּוֹךְ	midst; middle	תּוֹרָה	Torah
נוֹתֵן	giver of	אֱמֶת	truth
נָתַן	he gave	וְחַיֵּי עוֹלָם	and everlasting life

Knowing the Words
Circle the correct Hebrew word.

1. giver of	נָתַן	עוֹלָם	נוֹתֵן
2. in our midst	בְּתוֹכֵנוּ	אֱמֶת	בָּרוּר
3. he planted	בָּרוּךְ	אַתָּה	נָטַע
4. life	בְּתוֹכֵנוּ	חַיֵּי	נָתַן־לָנוּ
5. Torah	הַתּוֹרָה	נָטַע	תּוֹרָה
6. truth	אֱמֶת	תּוֹרַת	עוֹלָם
7. the Torah of	הָעוֹלָם	תּוֹרַת	וְחַיֵּי
8. to us	לָנוּ	אַתָּה	נוֹתֵן
9. he gave	בָּרוּר	נָתַן	אֲשֶׁר

In the Eastern European ghettos, when a child became five, and was considered ready for education, the father would proudly carry him on his shoulders through the town to the schoolroom.

Then the rabbi would open a *Humash* to the first page and with the child's forefinger would touch the first word of the תּוֹרָה, "בְּרֵאשִׁית" (in the beginning). The father would then put a drop of honey on the child's finger and place it in the youngster's mouth. In this way, the child's first contact with תּוֹרָה and learning was made sweet.

The second blessing is chanted after the Torah portion has been read. In it we thank God for giving a Torah of truth, because it has given us everlasting life. As long as the Torah lives and its teachings are practiced, the Jewish people will also live.

Blessed are You, Eternal,   בָּרוּךְ אַתָּה יְיָ,
     our God, ruler of the world,   אֱלֹהֵינוּ מֶלֶךְ הָעוֹלָם,
     who gave us the Torah of truth,   אֲשֶׁר נָתַן־לָנוּ תּוֹרַת אֱמֶת,
     and planted everlasting life   וְחַיֵּי עוֹלָם נָטַע בְּתוֹכֵנוּ.
         in our midst.
Blessed is the Eternal,   בָּרוּךְ אַתָּה יְיָ,
     giver of the Torah.   נוֹתֵן הַתּוֹרָה.

Knowing the Phrases
Draw a line from the Hebrew phrase to its English meaning.

1. Blessed are You, Eternal   אֲשֶׁר נָתַן־לָנוּ תּוֹרַת אֱמֶת
2. giver of the Torah   וְחַיֵּי עוֹלָם נָטַע בְּתוֹכֵנוּ
3. who gave us the Torah of truth   נוֹתֵן הַתּוֹרָה
4. and planted everlasting life in our midst   בָּרוּךְ אַתָּה יְיָ

The reader reads the תוֹרָה portion. At the end of the reading, the honoree closes the תוֹרָה and recites this blessing.

בָּרוּךְ אַתָּה יְיָ, אֱלֹהֵינוּ מֶלֶךְ הָעוֹלָם, אֲשֶׁר נָתַן לָנוּ תּוֹרַת אֱמֶת, וְחַיֵּי עוֹלָם נָטַע בְּתוֹכֵנוּ. בָּרוּךְ אַתָּה יְיָ, נוֹתֵן הַתּוֹרָה.

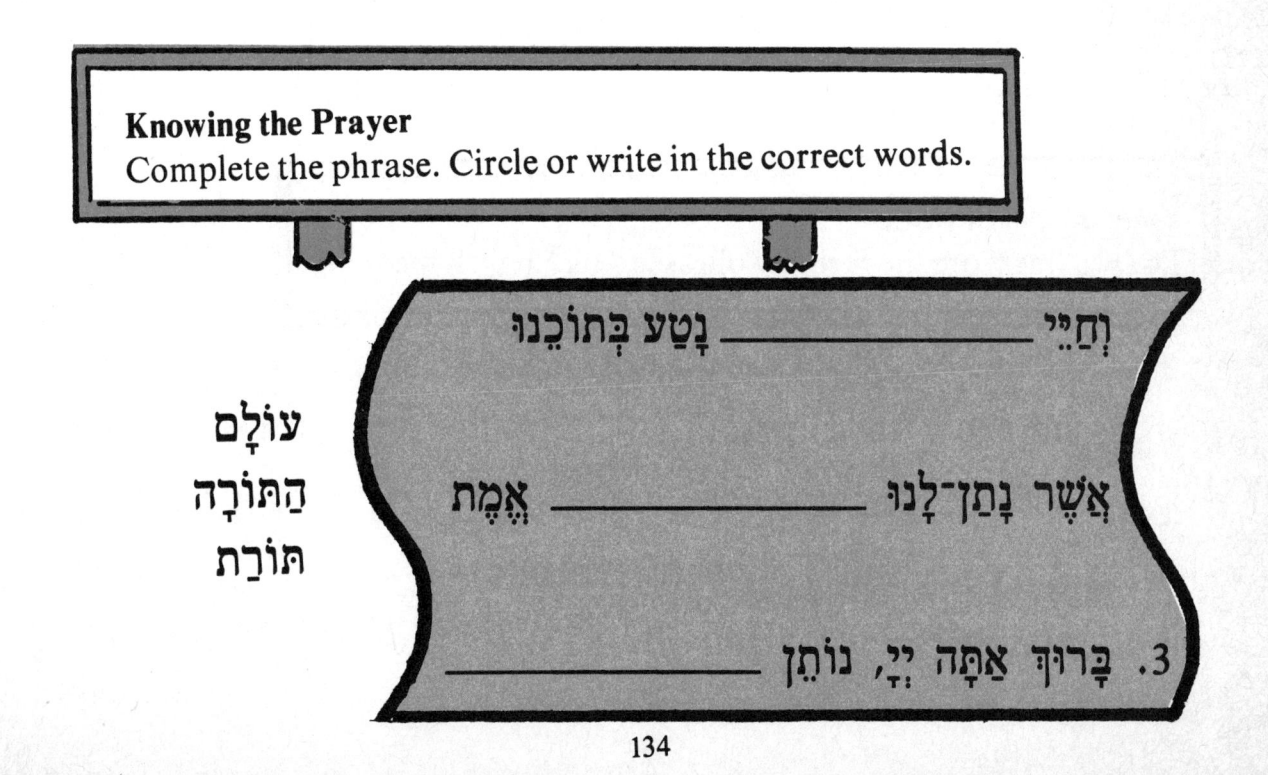

Knowing the Prayer
Complete the phrase. Circle or write in the correct words.

וְחַיֵּי _____ נָטַע בְּתוֹכֵנוּ

עוֹלָם
הַתּוֹרָה
תּוֹרַת

אֲשֶׁר נָתַן־לָנוּ _____ אֱמֶת

3. בָּרוּךְ אַתָּה יְיָ, נוֹתֵן _____

Knowing the Answers
Write your answer to the questions.

1. What is meant by "Torah of truth"?
   _____
   _____

2. Why do we thank the Eternal for giving us the Torah?
   _____
   _____

Knowing the Suffixes
Fill in the missing translations.

1. אֱלֹהִים means God   אֱלֹהֵינוּ means our God

2. עוֹלָם means _____   עוֹלָמֵנוּ means _____

3. תּוֹרָה means _____   תּוֹרָתֵנוּ means _____

4. מֶלֶךְ means _____   מַלְכֵּנוּ means _____

The suffix נוּ at the end of a word means _____.

עֲשֶׂרֶת הַדִּבְּרוֹת
The Ten Commandments

Right after Moses led the Children of Israel out of Egypt, he heard the voice of God telling him to go to the top of Mount Sinai. Moses stayed on the mountaintop for forty days and forty nights. When he came back down to the people, he brought with him two stone tablets. Written on the tablets were ten great laws which God had given him. These were the Ten Commandments.

The Ten Commandments are the most famous laws in the whole world. And if the whole world lived up to these great laws, everyone would be happy and there would always be peace.

1. I am the Lord your God who brought you out of the land of Egypt, out of the house of bondage.
2. You shall have no other gods before Me.
3. You shall not take the name of the Lord your God in vain.
4. Remember the Sabbath day to keep it holy.
5. Honor your father and mother.
6. You shall not murder.
7. You shall not commit adultery.
8. You shall not steal.
9. You shall not bear false witness.
10. You shall not envy.

When we recite the Torah blessing and thank God "for giving us the Torah of Truth," we are also thanking God for giving us the Ten Commandments.

The eighth and ninth commandments tell us "Thou shalt not steal" and "Thou shalt not bear false witness." This means that stealing and lying are wrong, and being honest and truthful is right. אֱמֶת is one way we have of showing that we are special and different from animals, that we are more like God.

Animals don't know the difference between right and wrong. A big dog will grab a bone away from a puppy. He doesn't even know he is doing something wrong. But you and I don't grab what belongs to someone else, even if the other person is smaller than we are. We do not lie to our parents, friends, or teachers. We know the difference between right and wrong.

Our wise men tell us that where there is אֱמֶת there is God.

The letters in אֱמֶת remind us that God is first, last, and ever present.

א is the first letter in the alefbet, מ is the middle letter, and ת is the last letter.

The tiny bit of God inside us tells us that what is אֱמֶת makes us feel wonderful and special. When we are special, we are less like the animals and more like God.

The Truthful Musical Scale

People who know the difference between the truth and the lie want to be fair. When we are fair, we are helping to make the world better.

Following are the notes of the אמת Musical Scale. Write about the time you or someone you know was truthful, to each note on the Musical Scale.

Do—Something I DO not _____.

Re—I REmembered to _____.

Me—The tiME I _____.

Fa—Everyone in my FAmily _____.

So—SOmething I did to help _____.

La—A time I was pLAying and _____.

Ti—The TIme I went to the store _____.

138

עֵץ חַיִּים הִיא
A Tree of Life

Knowning the Prayer Vocabulary

תָּמַךְ	he supported	עֵץ	tree
מְאֻשָּׁר	are happy	חַיִּים	life
דְּרָכֶיהָ	its ways	הִיא	she
דֶּרֶךְ	way, road	לַמַּחֲזִיקִים	to those who grasp
דַּרְכֵי נֹעַם	pleasant ways	הֶחֱזִיק	he grasped
נְתִיבוֹתֶיהָ	its paths	בָּהּ	it
נָתִיב	path, road	וְתוֹמְכֶיהָ	and those who support it

Knowing the Words
Circle the correct Hebrew.

1. to those who grasp	חַיִּים	וְתוֹמְכֶיהָ	לַמַּחֲזִיקִים	
2. she	הַגֶּפֶן	הִיא	עֵץ	
3. life	נְתִיבוֹ	הָעוֹלָם	חַיִּים	
4. tree	עֵץ	דְּרָכֶיהָ	מְאֻשָּׁר	
5. its paths	דְּרָכֶיהָ	שָׁלוֹם	לַמַּחֲזִיקִים	
6. way, road	בָּהּ	דֶּרֶךְ	הִיא	
7. pleasant ways	הִיא	לַמַּחֲזִיקִים	דַּרְכֵי־נֹעַם	
8. its ways	נְתִיבוֹתֶיהָ	שָׁלוֹם	מְאֻשָּׁר	
9. are happy, happiness	מְאֻשָּׁר	דְּרָכֶיהָ	וְתוֹמְכֶיהָ	
10. and those who support it	עֵץ	וְתוֹמְכֶיהָ	דַּרְכֵי־נֹעַם	

After reading the סִדְרָה, the סֵפֶר תּוֹרָה is held up and we say the following prayer in which we remind ourselves that the תּוֹרָה was given by God to Moses in the presence of all the Children of Israel:

The Torah is a tree of life	עֵץ חַיִּים הִיא
to those who grasp it,	לַמַּחֲזִיקִים בָּהּ
and those who support it are happy.	וְתוֹמְכֶיהָ מְאֻשָּׁר.
Its ways are pleasant ways,	דְּרָכֶיהָ דַרְכֵי־נֹעַם,
and all its paths are peace.	וְכָל־נְתִיבוֹתֶיהָ שָׁלוֹם.

Knowing the Phrases
Draw a line from the Hebrew phrase to its English meaning.

1. and those who support it are happy   עֵץ חַיִּים הִיא

2. and all its paths are peace   לַמַּחֲזִיקִים בָּהּ

3. the Torah is a tree of life   וְתוֹמְכֶיהָ מְאֻשָּׁר

4. to those who grasp it,   וְכָל־נְתִיבוֹתֶיהָ שָׁלוֹם

The Torah is our עֵץ חַיִּים. If we obey its rules, our lives will be fruitful and filled with happiness.

עֵץ חַיִּים הִיא לַמַּחֲזִיקִים בָּהּ, וְתֹמְכֶיהָ מְאֻשָּׁר.
דְּרָכֶיהָ דַרְכֵי נֹעַם, וְכָל נְתִיבוֹתֶיהָ שָׁלוֹם.

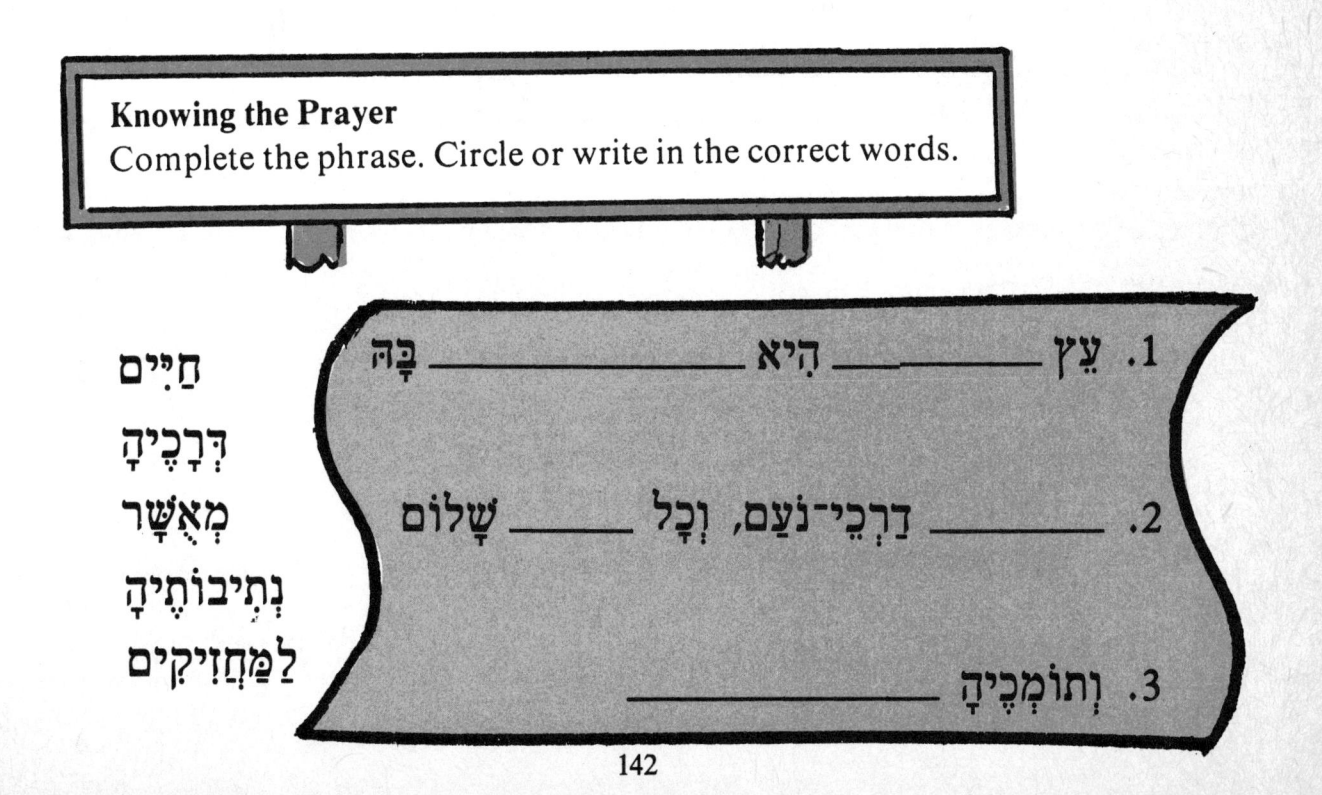

Knowing the Prayer
Complete the phrase. Circle or write in the correct words.

חַיִּים
דְּרָכֶיהָ
מְאֻשָּׁר
נְתִיבוֹתֶיהָ
לַמַּחֲזִיקִים

1. עֵץ _____ הִיא _____ בָּהּ

2. _____ דַּרְכֵי־נֹעַם, וְכָל _____ שָׁלוֹם

3. וְתוֹמְכֶיהָ _____

Knowing the Answers
Write your answer to the questions.

1. How can the Torah be a tree of life?
   _____
   _____

2. Can the Torah make you happy?
   _____
   _____

3. How can the teachings of the Torah lead to peace?
   _____
   _____

Knowing the Suffixes
Fill in the missing words.

1. דְּרָכִים means ways, roads   דְּרָכֶיהָ means its way, its roads

2. דְּבָרִים means _____   דְּבָרֶיהָ means _____

3. מִצְווֹת means _____   מִצְווֹתֶיהָ means _____

The suffix ֶיהָ at the end of a word means _____ .

עַם הַסֵּפֶר
The People of the Book

How different the world would be without books! If there were no books, we would still be living in caves and hunting with bows and arrows. Life would be very dull and just no fun at all.

The learning in books is passed down through the years. People learn and write what they learn in books. After they die, other people come along and learn what is written in the books. These people also write books. As time goes on, there are more and more books for everyone to read and learn from. From books, scientists learn and make new discoveries like atomic energy, laser beams, jet flying, and space ships. Doctors learn from books and make great new discoveries in medicine.

Over 3,000 years ago, a great book started the Jewish people off on their long road of learning. That book is the Torah. All those thousands of years the Jewish people loved learning. Jews even look upon their prayers as study and learning. Every Saturday in the synagogues and every holiday, a part of the Torah is read. The services every morning, afternoon, and evening contain study portions from the Torah, the Talmud, and the Mishna.

No wonder the Jews are known as עַם הַסֵּפֶר ("people of the book"). Out of 220 Nobel Prize winners, 45 have been Jews. This is because of the Jews' love and respect for books, learning, and study. The Torah and all the other great books have helped give the Jews great heroes and scientists. These are the people who have taught Jews through the ages to live lives of peace, justice, and service to humanity.

What Do You Think?
1. What is the Nobel Prize? How did it get its name?
2. What is a printing press?
3. How were books written before the printing press was invented?
4. How do books help us learn? What book started the Jewish people on their road to learning?
5. How can a book help make you a better person?
6. How can Torah help you become a better Jew? A better person?

הַבְדָלָה
Havdalah

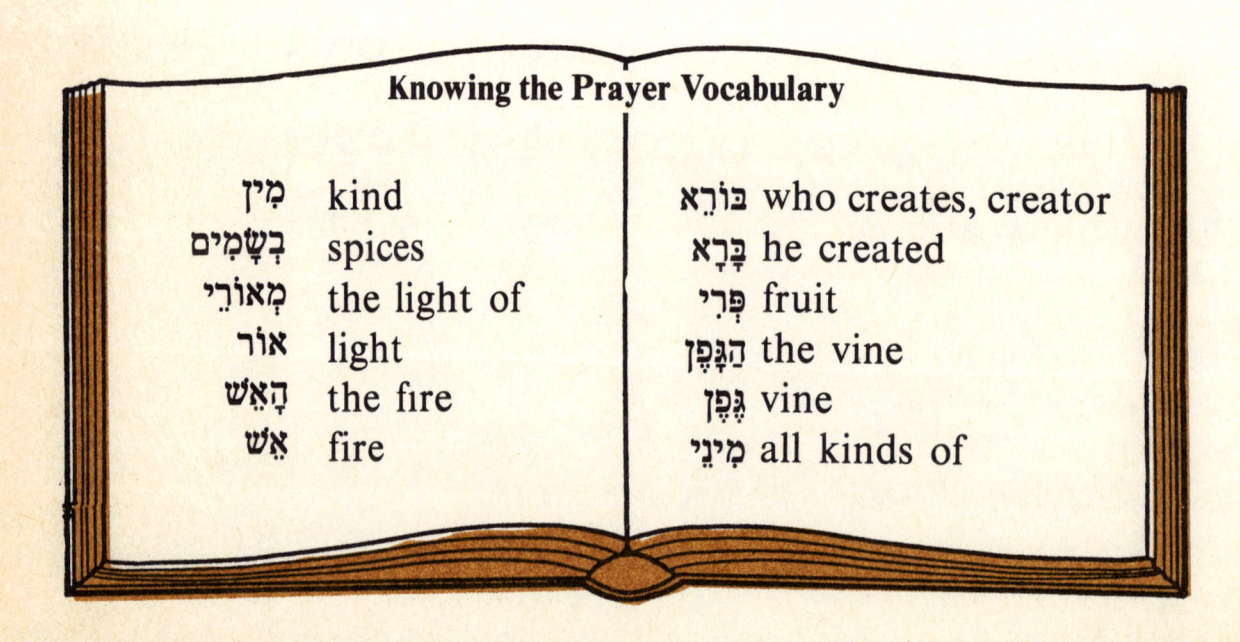

Knowing the Prayer Vocabulary

מִין	kind	בּוֹרֵא	who creates, creator
בְּשָׂמִים	spices	בָּרָא	he created
מְאוֹרֵי	the light of	פְּרִי	fruit
אוֹר	light	הַגֶּפֶן	the vine
הָאֵשׁ	the fire	גֶּפֶן	vine
אֵשׁ	fire	מִינֵי	all kinds of

145

Knowing the Words
Circle the correct Hebrew word.

1. all kinds of	אֱלֹהֵינוּ	מֶלֶךְ	מִינֵי
2. kind	מֶלֶךְ	מִין	פְּרִי
3. spices	אֱלֹהֵינוּ	בָּרוּךְ	בְּשָׂמִים
4. the light of	אַתָּה	מְאוֹרֵי	הָאֵשׁ
5. light	אוֹר	אַתָּה	מְאוֹרֵי
6. the fire	הָעוֹלָם	הָאֵשׁ	מִינֵי
7. the vine	הַגֶּפֶן	בּוֹרֵא	מֶלֶךְ
8. he created	בָּרָא	אֱלֹהֵינוּ	בָּרוּךְ
9. fruit	בּוֹרֵא	בְּשָׂמִים	פְּרִי
10. who creates	בָּרוּךְ	אַתָּה	בּוֹרֵא

The end of Sabbath or a festival is marked by a ceremony of separation between the holy and the earthly. The קִדּוּשׁ begins the holy period; the הַבְדָּלָה ends it. Since קִדּוּשׁ requires יַיִן, the concluding בְּרָכוֹת are made over a glass of יַיִן and בְּשָׂמִים (spice) box. The third and last בְּרָכָה is recited over a lit הַבְדָּלָה candle because light was given the universe on the first day of creation.

Holding a cup of wine:

Blessed are You, Eternal,   בָּרוּךְ אַתָּה יְיָ,

our God, ruler of the world,   אֱלֹהֵינוּ מֶלֶךְ הָעוֹלָם,

who creates the fruit of the vine.   בּוֹרֵא פְּרִי הַגָּפֶן.

Over fragrant spices:

Blessed are You, Eternal,   בָּרוּךְ אַתָּה יְיָ,

our God, ruler of the world,   אֱלֹהֵינוּ מֶלֶךְ הָעוֹלָם,

who creates all kinds of spices.   בּוֹרֵא מִינֵי בְשָׂמִים.

Over a lit Havdalah candle:

Blessed are You, Eternal,   בָּרוּךְ אַתָּה יְיָ,

our God, ruler of the world,   אֱלֹהֵינוּ מֶלֶךְ הָעוֹלָם,

who creates the light of the fire.   בּוֹרֵא מְאוֹרֵי הָאֵשׁ.

Knowing the Phrases
Draw a line from the Hebrew phrase to its English meaning.

1. who creates all kinds of spices　　　　בּוֹרֵא פְּרִי הַגֶּפֶן

2. who creates the fruit of the vine　　　　בּוֹרֵא מְאוֹרֵי הָאֵשׁ

3. who creates the light of fire　　　　בּוֹרֵא מִינֵי בְשָׂמִים

Knowing the Prayer
Draw a line or write in the correct word.

1. בּוֹרֵא _____ הַגֶּפֶן

מְאוֹרֵי

מִינֵי　　2. בּוֹרֵא _____ בְשָׂמִים

פְּרִי

3. בּוֹרֵא _____ הָאֵשׁ

הַבְדָלָה is recited standing, with a cup of wine in the right hand and the בְּשָׂמִים in the left. After the בְּרָכָה over the wine, the בְּשָׂמִים are taken in the right hand. The aroma of the בְּשָׂמִים is inhaled as the בְּרָכָה is recited.
Then, both the wine and the בְּשָׂמִים are put down and the בְּרָכָה is recited over the lighted הַבְדָלָה.

Holding a cup of wine:

בָּרוּךְ אַתָּה יְיָ, אֱלֹהֵינוּ מֶלֶךְ הָעוֹלָם, בּוֹרֵא פְּרִי הַגָּפֶן.

Over fragrant spices:

בָּרוּךְ אַתָּה יְיָ, אֱלֹהֵינוּ מֶלֶךְ הָעוֹלָם, בּוֹרֵא מִינֵי בְשָׂמִים.

Over a lit Havdalah candle:

בָּרוּךְ אַתָּה יְיָ, אֱלֹהֵינוּ מֶלֶךְ הָעוֹלָם, בּוֹרֵא מְאוֹרֵי הָאֵשׁ.

Knowing the Prefixes
Fill in the missing translations.

1. אֵשׁ means fire   הָאֵשׁ means the fire
2. גֶּפֶן means _____   הַגֶּפֶן means _____
3. בְּשָׂמִים means _____   הַבְּשָׂמִים means _____
4. עוֹלָם means _____   הָעוֹלָם means _____
5. מֶלֶךְ means _____   הַמֶּלֶךְ means _____

The prefix הָ at the start of a word means _____

Knowing the Answers
Write your answer to the questions.

Each one of the *Havdalah* items appeals to one or more of our senses: smelling, tasting, hearing, touching, seeing.

1. To what senses does wine appeal?

   _____

   _____

2. To what senses do the spices appeal?

   _____

   _____

3. To what senses does the *Havdalah* candle appeal?

   _____

   _____

Knowing Siddur Facts.

שַׁבָּת is welcomed with the קִדּוּשׁ, which begins with the blessing over wine. The הַבְדָלָה ceremony also begins with the בְּרָכָה over wine.

הַבְדָּלָה
Havdalah

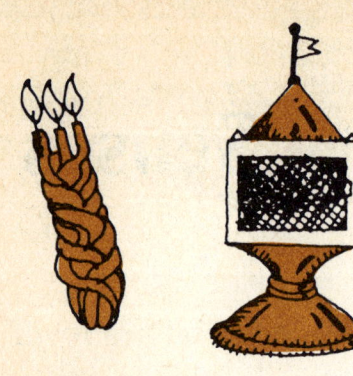

On Saturday night, when three stars twinkle in the sky, it is time to bring the Sabbath to a close with the הַבְדָּלָה ceremony. הַבְדָּלָה means "separation," for the ceremony separates the Sabbath from the weekday that is about to begin. The idea of separating or dividing things of one kind from things of another kind is a very important part of the creation. For example, the Torah tells us that on the second day of creation God separated (וַיַּבְדֵּל) the water above the רָקִיעַ from the waters below the רָקִיעַ. Later, God separates the Sabbath from the ordinary weekday, making it holy and sanctified. By separating something God makes it special and unique.

The הַבְדָּלָה ceremony is a beautiful way of saying goodbye to the Sabbath Queen. To make הַבְדָּלָה you need a cup of wine, a special candle (with four wicks), and fragrant spices. Each item that is used appeals to one of our senses—wine for our sense of taste, the candle for our sight, and the spices for our sense of smell. It is as if our senses need to be perked up and brought back to life to help us get over our sadness at the end of the beautiful Sabbath.

While someone holds the הַבְדָּלָה candle up high, another person holds the wine cup and recites the blessings over wine, spices, and light. Everyone repeats the blessings over spices and light and takes a turn smelling the spices and using the candlelight. At the end of the prayer, someone drinks the wine, and the Sabbath is over.

The Five Senses

God gave us five senses with which to appreciate the wonders and beauty of the world: hearing, seeing, touching, smelling, and tasting. All day long we use these marvelous gifts of God.

We taste the delicious foods of the world with our _____.
We smell the odors of the world with our _____.
We see the beauty of the world with our _____.
We hear the wonders of the world with our _____.
We touch the marvels of the world with our _____.
Think of some things you heard, smelled, touched, or saw today.

_____

_____

יָדַיִם   עֵינַיִם   לָשׁוֹן   אָזְנַיִם   אַף

קִדּוּשׁ לְלֵיל שַׁבָּת
KIDDUSH FOR FRIDAY NIGHT

1. וַיְהִי־עֶרֶב וַיְהִי־בֹקֶר
2. יוֹם הַשִּׁשִּׁי:
3. וַיְכֻלּוּ הַשָּׁמַיִם וְהָאָרֶץ וְכָל־צְבָאָם:
4. וַיְכַל אֱלֹהִים בַּיּוֹם הַשְּׁבִיעִי,
5. מְלַאכְתּוֹ אֲשֶׁר עָשָׂה:
6. וַיִּשְׁבֹּת בַּיּוֹם הַשְּׁבִיעִי מִכָּל מְלַאכְתּוֹ
7. אֲשֶׁר עָשָׂה:
8. וַיְבָרֶךְ אֱלֹהִים אֶת יוֹם הַשְּׁבִיעִי וַיְקַדֵּשׁ אֹתוֹ,
9. כִּי בוֹ שָׁבַת מִכָּל מְלַאכְתּוֹ,
10. אֲשֶׁר בָּרָא אֱלֹהִים לַעֲשׂוֹת:

On Wine: —	On Bread: —
11. סַבְרִי מָרָנָן וְרַבּוֹתַי:	סַבְרִי מָרָנָן וְרַבּוֹתַי:
12. בָּרוּךְ אַתָּה יְיָ,	בָּרוּךְ אַתָּה יְיָ,
13. אֱלֹהֵינוּ מֶלֶךְ הָעוֹלָם,	אֱלֹהֵינוּ מֶלֶךְ הָעוֹלָם,
14. בּוֹרֵא פְּרִי הַגָּפֶן:	הַמּוֹצִיא לֶחֶם מִן הָאָרֶץ:

1. בָּרוּךְ אַתָּה יְיָ, אֱלֹהֵינוּ מֶלֶךְ הָעוֹלָם.
2. אֲשֶׁר קִדְּשָׁנוּ בְּמִצְוֹתָיו וְרָצָה בָנוּ.
3. וְשַׁבַּת קָדְשׁוֹ, בְּאַהֲבָה וּבְרָצוֹן הִנְחִילָנוּ,
4. זִכָּרוֹן לְמַעֲשֵׂה בְרֵאשִׁית.
5. כִּי הוּא יוֹם, תְּחִלָּה לְמִקְרָאֵי קֹדֶשׁ,
6. זֵכֶר לִיצִיאַת מִצְרָיִם.
7. כִּי־בָנוּ בָחַרְתָּ, וְאוֹתָנוּ קִדַּשְׁתָּ מִכָּל הָעַמִּים.
8. וְשַׁבַּת קָדְשְׁךָ, בְּאַהֲבָה וּבְרָצוֹן הִנְחַלְתָּנוּ:
9. בָּרוּךְ אַתָּה יְיָ, מְקַדֵּשׁ הַשַּׁבָּת.

Reader and Cong.

1. לְכָה דוֹדִי לִקְרַאת כַּלָּה.
2. פְּנֵי שַׁבָּת נְקַבְּלָה: לְכָה דוֹדִי

Cong. and Reader

3. שָׁמוֹר וְזָכוֹר בְּדִבּוּר אֶחָד.
4. הִשְׁמִיעָנוּ אֵל הַמְיֻחָד.
5. יְיָ אֶחָד וּשְׁמוֹ אֶחָד.
6. לְשֵׁם וּלְתִפְאֶרֶת וְלִתְהִלָּה:
7. לְכָה דוֹדִי לִקְרַאת כַּלָּה.
8. פְּנֵי שַׁבָּת נְקַבְּלָה:

Cong. and Reader

9. לִקְרַאת שַׁבָּת לְכוּ וְנֵלְכָה.
10. כִּי הִיא מְקוֹר הַבְּרָכָה.
11. מֵרֹאשׁ מִקֶּדֶם נְסוּכָה.
12. סוֹף מַעֲשֶׂה בְּמַחֲשָׁבָה תְּחִלָּה:
13. לְכָה דוֹדִי לִקְרַאת כַּלָּה.
14. פְּנֵי שַׁבָּת נְקַבְּלָה:

Cong. and Reader

1. מִקְדַּשׁ מֶלֶךְ עִיר מְלוּכָה.
2. קוּמִי צְאִי מִתּוֹךְ הַהֲפֵכָה.
3. רַב לָךְ שֶׁבֶת בְּעֵמֶק הַבָּכָא.
4. וְהוּא יַחֲמֹל עָלַיִךְ חֶמְלָה:
5. לְכָה דוֹדִי לִקְרַאת כַּלָּה.
6. פְּנֵי שַׁבָּת נְקַבְּלָה:

Cong. and Reader

7. הִתְנַעֲרִי מֵעָפָר, קוּמִי.
8. לִבְשִׁי בִּגְדֵי תִפְאַרְתֵּךְ, עַמִּי.
9. עַל־יַד בֶּן יִשַׁי בֵּית הַלַּחְמִי.
10. קָרְבָה אֶל נַפְשִׁי גְאָלָהּ:
11. לְכָה דוֹדִי לִקְרַאת כַּלָּה.
12. פְּנֵי שַׁבָּת נְקַבְּלָה:

1. אֵל מֶלֶךְ נֶאֱמָן.

2. שְׁמַע יִשְׂרָאֵל, יְיָ אֱלֹהֵינוּ, יְיָ אֶחָד:

3. בָּרוּךְ שֵׁם כְּבוֹד מַלְכוּתוֹ לְעוֹלָם וָעֶד.

4. וְאָהַבְתָּ אֵת יְיָ אֱלֹהֶיךָ, בְּכָל־לְבָבְךָ, וּבְכָל

5. נַפְשְׁךָ, וּבְכָל־מְאֹדֶךָ: וְהָיוּ הַדְּבָרִים הָאֵלֶּה,

6. אֲשֶׁר אָנֹכִי מְצַוְּךָ הַיּוֹם, עַל־לְבָבֶךָ: וְשִׁנַּנְתָּם

7. לְבָנֶיךָ, וְדִבַּרְתָּ בָּם, בְּשִׁבְתְּךָ בְּבֵיתֶךָ,

8. וּבְלֶכְתְּךָ בַדֶּרֶךְ, וּבְשָׁכְבְּךָ וּבְקוּמֶךָ:

9. וּקְשַׁרְתָּם לְאוֹת עַל־יָדֶךָ, וְהָיוּ לְטֹטָפֹת בֵּין

10. עֵינֶיךָ: וּכְתַבְתָּם עַל־מְזֻזוֹת בֵּיתֶךָ וּבִשְׁעָרֶיךָ:

11. וְהָיָה אִם שָׁמֹעַ תִּשְׁמְעוּ אֶל־מִצְוֹתַי, אֲשֶׁר

12. אָנֹכִי מְצַוֶּה אֶתְכֶם הַיּוֹם, לְאַהֲבָה אֶת־יְיָ

13. אֱלֹהֵיכֶם וּלְעָבְדוֹ, בְּכָל־לְבַבְכֶם וּבְכָל

14. נַפְשְׁכֶם: וְנָתַתִּי מְטַר־אַרְצְכֶם בְּעִתּוֹ, יוֹרֶה

15. וּמַלְקוֹשׁ, וְאָסַפְתָּ דְגָנֶךָ וְתִירֹשְׁךָ וְיִצְהָרֶךָ:

1 וְנָתַתִּי עֵשֶׂב בְּשָׂדְךָ לִבְהֶמְתֶּךָ, וְאָכַלְתָּ
2 וְשָׂבָעְתָּ: הִשָּׁמְרוּ לָכֶם פֶּן־יִפְתֶּה לְבַבְכֶם,
3 וְסַרְתֶּם וַעֲבַדְתֶּם אֱלֹהִים אֲחֵרִים
4 וְהִשְׁתַּחֲוִיתֶם לָהֶם: וְחָרָה אַף־יְיָ בָּכֶם,
5 וְעָצַר אֶת־הַשָּׁמַיִם וְלֹא יִהְיֶה מָטָר, וְהָאֲדָמָה
6 לֹא תִתֵּן אֶת־יְבוּלָהּ, וַאֲבַדְתֶּם מְהֵרָה מֵעַל
7 הָאָרֶץ הַטֹּבָה, אֲשֶׁר יְיָ נֹתֵן לָכֶם: וְשַׂמְתֶּם
8 אֶת־דְּבָרַי אֵלֶּה עַל־לְבַבְכֶם וְעַל־נַפְשְׁכֶם,
9 וּקְשַׁרְתֶּם אֹתָם לְאוֹת עַל־יֶדְכֶם, וְהָיוּ
10 לְטוֹטָפֹת בֵּין עֵינֵיכֶם: וְלִמַּדְתֶּם אֹתָם אֶת־
11 בְּנֵיכֶם, לְדַבֵּר בָּם, בְּשִׁבְתְּךָ בְּבֵיתֶךָ,
12 וּבְלֶכְתְּךָ בַדֶּרֶךְ, וּבְשָׁכְבְּךָ וּבְקוּמֶךָ:
13 וּכְתַבְתָּם עַל מְזוּזוֹת בֵּיתֶךָ וּבִשְׁעָרֶיךָ: לְמַעַן
14 יִרְבּוּ יְמֵיכֶם וִימֵי בְנֵיכֶם עַל הָאֲדָמָה,
15 אֲשֶׁר נִשְׁבַּע יְיָ לַאֲבֹתֵיכֶם לָתֵת לָהֶם, כִּימֵי
16 הַשָּׁמַיִם עַל הָאָרֶץ:

1. עָלֵינוּ לְשַׁבֵּחַ לַאֲדוֹן הַכֹּל, לָתֵת גְּדֻלָּה
2. לְיוֹצֵר בְּרֵאשִׁית, שֶׁלֹּא עָשָׂנוּ כְּגוֹיֵי הָאֲרָצוֹת,
3. וְלֹא שָׂמָנוּ כְּמִשְׁפְּחוֹת הָאֲדָמָה, שֶׁלֹּא שָׂם
4. חֶלְקֵנוּ כָּהֶם וְגוֹרָלֵנוּ כְּכָל הֲמוֹנָם.
5. וַאֲנַחְנוּ כֹּרְעִים וּמִשְׁתַּחֲוִים וּמוֹדִים לִפְנֵי
6. מֶלֶךְ מַלְכֵי הַמְּלָכִים, הַקָּדוֹשׁ, בָּרוּךְ
7. הוּא. שֶׁהוּא נוֹטֶה שָׁמַיִם וְיוֹסֵד אָרֶץ, וּמוֹשַׁב
8. יְקָרוֹ בַּשָּׁמַיִם מִמַּעַל וּשְׁכִינַת עֻזּוֹ בְּגָבְהֵי
9. מְרוֹמִים, הוּא אֱלֹהֵינוּ אֵין עוֹד. אֱמֶת –
10. מַלְכֵּנוּ, אֶפֶס זוּלָתוֹ, כַּכָּתוּב בְּתוֹרָתוֹ:
11. "וְיָדַעְתָּ הַיּוֹם וַהֲשֵׁבֹתָ אֶל לְבָבֶךָ, כִּי יְיָ
12. הוּא הָאֱלֹהִים בַּשָּׁמַיִם מִמַּעַל וְעַל הָאָרֶץ
13. מִתָּחַת, אֵין עוֹד".

Upon entering the synagogue say:

1. מַה־טֹּבוּ אֹהָלֶיךָ, יַעֲקֹב,
2. מִשְׁכְּנֹתֶיךָ יִשְׂרָאֵל.
3. וַאֲנִי, בְּרֹב חַסְדְּךָ, אָבֹא בֵיתֶךָ,
4. אֶשְׁתַּחֲוֶה אֶל הֵיכַל קָדְשְׁךָ בְּיִרְאָתֶךָ.
5. יְיָ, אָהַבְתִּי מְעוֹן בֵּיתֶךָ,
6. וּמְקוֹם מִשְׁכַּן כְּבוֹדֶךָ.
7. וַאֲנִי אֶשְׁתַּחֲוֶה וְאֶכְרָעָה,
8. אֶבְרְכָה לִפְנֵי יְיָ עֹשִׂי.
9. וַאֲנִי תְפִלָּתִי לְךָ יְיָ, עֵת רָצוֹן,
10. אֱלֹהִים, בְּרָב־חַסְדֶּךָ, עֲנֵנִי בֶּאֱמֶת יִשְׁעֶךָ.